INTRODUCING
ISSUES WITH
OPPOSING
VIEWPOINTS®

Teen
Driving

Mary E. Williams, *Book Editor*

GREENHAVEN PRESS
A part of Gale, Cengage Learning

GALE
CENGAGE Learning·

Detroit • New York • San Francisco • New Haven, Conn • Waterville, Maine • London

Elizabeth Des Chenes, *Director, Content Strategy*
Cynthia Sanner, *Publisher*
Douglas Dentino, *Manager, New Product*

© 2014 Greenhaven Press, a part of Gale, Cengage Learning

WCN: 01-100-101

For more information, contact:
Greenhaven Press
27500 Drake Rd.
Farmington Hills, MI 48331-3535
Or you can visit our Internet site at gale.cengage.com

For product information and technology assistance, contact us at

Gale Customer Support, 1-800-877-4253
For permission to use material from this text or product, submit all requests online at www.cengage.com/permissions

Further permissions questions can be e-mailed to permissionrequest@cengage.com

Articles in Greenhaven Press anthologies are often edited for length to meet page requirements. In addition, original titles of these works are changed to clearly present the main thesis and to explicitly indicate the author's opinion. Every effort is made to ensure that Greenhaven Press accurately reflects the original intent of the authors. Every effort has been made to trace the owners of copyrighted material.

LIBRARY OF CONGRESS CATALOGING-IN-PUBLICATION DATA

Teen driving / Mary E. Williams, book editor.
    pages cm. -- (Introducing issues with opposing viewpoints)
Includes bibliographical references and index.
ISBN 978-0-7377-4943-4 (hardcover)
1. Teenage automobile drivers--United States--Juvenile literature. I. Williams, Mary E., 1960-
HE5620.J8T4383 2014
629.28'308350973--dc23
                         2013033395

Printed in the United States of America
1 2 3 4 5 6 7 18 17 16 15 14

Contents

Chapter 3: What Strategies Would Make Teen Driving Safer?

Foreword

Indulging in a wide spectrum of ideas, beliefs, and perspectives is a critical cornerstone of democracy. After all, it is often debates over differences of opinion, such as whether to legalize abortion, how to treat prisoners, or when to enact the death penalty, that shape our society and drive it forward. Such diversity of thought is frequently regarded as the hallmark of a healthy and civilized culture. As the Reverend Clifford Schutjer of the First Congregational Church in Mansfield, Ohio, declared in a 2001 sermon, "Surrounding oneself with only like-minded people, restricting what we listen to or read only to what we find agreeable is irresponsible. Refusing to entertain doubts once we make up our minds is a subtle but deadly form of arrogance." With this advice in mind, Introducing Issues with Opposing Viewpoints books aim to open readers' minds to the critically divergent views that comprise our world's most important debates.

Introducing Issues with Opposing Viewpoints simplifies for students the enormous and often overwhelming mass of material now available via print and electronic media. Collected in every volume is an array of opinions that captures the essence of a particular controversy or topic. Introducing Issues with Opposing Viewpoints books embody the spirit of nineteenth-century journalist Charles A. Dana's axiom: "Fight for your opinions, but do not believe that they contain the whole truth, or the only truth." Absorbing such contrasting opinions teaches students to analyze the strength of an argument and compare it to its opposition. From this process readers can inform and strengthen their own opinions, or be exposed to new information that will change their minds. Introducing Issues with Opposing Viewpoints is a mosaic of different voices. The authors are statesmen, pundits, academics, journalists, corporations, and ordinary people who have felt compelled to share their experiences and ideas in a public forum. Their words have been collected from newspapers, journals, books, speeches, interviews, and the Internet, the fastest growing body of opinionated material in the world.

Introducing Issues with Opposing Viewpoints shares many of the well-known features of its critically acclaimed parent series, Opposing Viewpoints. The articles are presented in a pro/con format, allowing readers to absorb divergent perspectives side by side. Active reading questions preface each viewpoint, requiring the student to approach the material thoughtfully and carefully. Useful charts, graphs, and cartoons supplement each article. A thorough introduction provides readers with crucial background on an issue. An annotated bibliography points the reader toward articles, books, and websites that contain additional information on the topic. An appendix of organizations to contact contains a wide variety of charities, nonprofit organizations, political groups, and private enterprises that each hold a position on the issue at hand. Finally, a comprehensive index allows readers to locate content quickly and efficiently.

Introducing Issues with Opposing Viewpoints is also significantly different from Opposing Viewpoints. As the series title implies, its presentation will help introduce students to the concept of opposing viewpoints and learn to use this material to aid in critical writing and debate. The series' four-color, accessible format makes the books attractive and inviting to readers of all levels. In addition, each viewpoint has been carefully edited to maximize a reader's understanding of the content. Short but thorough viewpoints capture the essence of an argument. A substantial, thought-provoking essay question placed at the end of each viewpoint asks the student to further investigate the issues raised in the viewpoint, compare and contrast two authors' arguments, or consider how one might go about forming an opinion on the topic at hand. Each viewpoint contains sidebars that include at-a-glance information and handy statistics. A Facts About section located in the back of the book further supplies students with relevant facts and figures.

Following in the tradition of the Opposing Viewpoints series, Greenhaven Press continues to provide readers with invaluable exposure to the controversial issues that shape our world. As John Stuart Mill once wrote: "The only way in which a human being can make some approach to knowing the whole of a subject is by hearing what can be said about it by persons of every variety of opinion and studying all modes in which it can be looked at by every character of mind. No wise man ever acquired his wisdom in any mode but this." It is to this principle that Introducing Issues with Opposing Viewpoints books are dedicated.

Introduction

At a high school in Nashville, Tennessee, seventeen-year-old Andrew (not his real name) has already sent more than two hundred text messages by the time he sits down for lunch. With his day beginning at 7:00 AM, that is an average of one text every ninety seconds.

Andrew's parents, teachers, and others far removed from their adolescent years tend to find this rate of texting unbelievable. But for "digital natives" like Andrew—those born during the age of digital technology and familiar with computers and the Internet from a young age—constant texting usually feels normal and natural. In Andrew's view, sending hundreds of texts by noon makes perfect sense. With a packed schedule that includes a part-time job at the local library, playing in a band, an internship organizing a trek to Latin America, daily classes, and studying, texting is quicker and more efficient than talking on the phone. As communications researchers Alice Marwick and Danah Boyd note, "Texting has become [Andrew's] lifeline. He texts his boss if he's going to be late, texts his coworkers to check out what's happening at work, and texts his friends and his girlfriend, who is away at college. For Andrew, as for so many teens, technology is a means to achieve both practical and social goals."[1]

Texting and other forms of social media, then, are an essential part of teen culture in most industrialized nations. Youths are generally better than adults at managing electronic tasks—they have a greater digital fluency than do those of older generations. Yet, teens are not very adept at dividing their attention between electronic tasks and other skills that require focus and risk assessment. While "multitasking" can be a challenge for anyone, it often involves an extra level of difficulty for teens. For this reason, researchers say, driving for teens who are digital natives involves dangers that previous generations of youths did not face.

The human brain takes more than twenty years to fully grow. The prefrontal cortex, which is the last region of the brain to develop, is responsible for decision making and for gauging the consequences of one's actions. Moreover, the neuronal "wiring" that manages impulse control seems to form the most slowly, notes Robert D. Foss, director of the University of North Carolina Center for the Study of Young Drivers. This is one reason why teens may speed or text while driving even though they are fully aware of how dangerous these actions can be. "I don't mean to say that we can excuse teenagers for irresponsible behavior," Foss points out. "They must be held accountable. But we can't blame them or talk them out of this development phase any more than we can talk a 2-year-old out of going through the Terrible Twos."[2]

Crash rates for teen drivers are nearly four times higher than for adult drivers, according to AAA (the American Automobile Association). Teens' lack of driving experience, along with their inability to divide their attention between different kinds of tasks, makes distracted driving (driving while one's attention is divided among different tasks or disruptions) even more risky for them than for adults. Researcher Bruce Simons-Morton conducted a study in which adults and teen drivers were asked to perform a specific task on a cell phone while driving on a test track. When the drivers came close to an intersection, the traffic signal turned yellow. All of the adults looked up from the cell phones and stopped at the light, but only 66 percent of the teens did so. Teens may perform both tasks well, but they are not as good at separating the tasks and watching the road.

The combination of frequent texting and poor impulse control in the teen brain creates a troubling scenario for youths who are novice drivers. Indeed, activities such as texting or adjusting an MP3 player are major causes of accidents among teen drivers; even conscientious youths like Andrew are not immune to crash-inducing distractions. However, traffic-safety experts are developing new tools to reduce the crash rate among digital natives. The San Francisco company Posit Science, for example, is creating video games that help teens practice the skills needed to manage the demands of driving even before they begin learning to drive. According to Posit Science's research and development director, Peter Delahunt, the games enable the neural connections in the prefrontal cortex to reorganize in a way that improves vision and attention. "Our approach helps people train their brains so they can process information faster and maintain focus on the road—and that makes them safer drivers,"[3] Delahunt contends. Engineer Xuesong Zhou has developed a completely different kind of tool: an ignition key that prevents cell phone use while the vehicle is running. To start the engine, the driver has to release a switch on the key that blocks all nonemergency use of the cell phone. "Using our system," explains Zhou, "you can prove that teens are not talking [or texting] while driving, which can significantly reduce the risk of getting into a car accident."[4]

Technology itself may very well provide some valuable solutions to the challenges faced by technologically savvy teen drivers today. How to make driving safer for teenagers is just one of the questions explored in *Introducing Issues with Opposing Viewpoints: Teen Driving.* Contributors also offer differing opinions on driver education, the minimum age for driving, the graduated driver's license, and related concerns. Everyone who is—or knows—a teen driver will find this volume informative and timely.

Notes

1. Alice Marwick and Danah Boyd, "Teens Text More than Adults, but They're Still Just Teens," *Daily Beast,* May 20, 2012. www .thedailybeast.com/newsweek/2012/05/20/teens-text-more-than -adults-but-they-re-still-just-teens.html.
2. Quoted in Kristen A. Nelson, "The Teen Brain: Under Construction," *Westways,* November–December 2012, p. 54.
3. Quoted in Nelson, *Westways,* p. 55.
4. Quoted in Newswise, "Car Key Jams Teen Drivers' Cell Phones and Texting," December 18, 2008. www.newswise.com/articles /car-key-jams-teen-drivers-cell-phones-and-texting.

Chapter 1

What Are the Risks Involved with Teen Driving?

There are increased risks involved when teens drive cars.

Viewpoint

1

US Teen Driving Deaths Are Surging

"One has to wonder whether there's a relationship between the increase in fatalities and the decrease in school-based driver-ed training."

Gregg Laskoski

There has been an increase in the number of sixteen- and seventeen-year-old driver deaths, asserts Gregg Laskoski in the following viewpoint. The increase in teen driver deaths coincides with a projection from the National Highway Traffic Safety Administration (NHTSA) in which all traffic deaths increased by 8 percent. It is concerning that teen drivers appear to be most impacted. Laskoski is a former news reporter (Gannett Westchester Newspapers New York) and has also worked for AAA (American Automobile Association), communicating with reporters daily on fuel price trends since 2002. He joined the GasBuddy Organization in 2011 and is based in Tampa, Florida.

AS YOU READ, CONSIDER THE FOLLOWING QUESTIONS:

1. According to a 2012 report cited by Laskoski, deaths of sixteen-year-old drivers increased from eighty-six to what?
2. According to the author, how many states reported increases in teen-driver deaths?
3. In Laskoski's opinion, what is one possible reason for the increase in teen-driver deaths?

A report released by the Governors Highway Safety Association (GHSA) reveals that the number of 16- and 17-year-old driver deaths in passenger vehicles increased dramatically for the first six months of 2012, based on preliminary data supplied by all 50 states and the District of Columbia. Overall, 16- and 17-year-old driver deaths increased from 202 to 240—a 19 percent jump.

FAST FACT

Car crashes are the leading cause of death among teens in the United States.

The increase in teen driver deaths coincides with a projection from the National Highway Traffic Safety Administration (NHTSA) in which all traffic deaths increased by 8 percent. It is particularly concerning that 16- and 17-year-old driver deaths appear to have increased at an even greater rate.

What will it take to convince our teens of the importance of safety and risk avoidance?

The new report—the first state-by-state look at teen driver fatalities in 2012—was completed by Dr. Allan Williams, a researcher

Drivers between the ages of fifteen and twenty-four (especially males) have the highest rate of auto-related deaths.

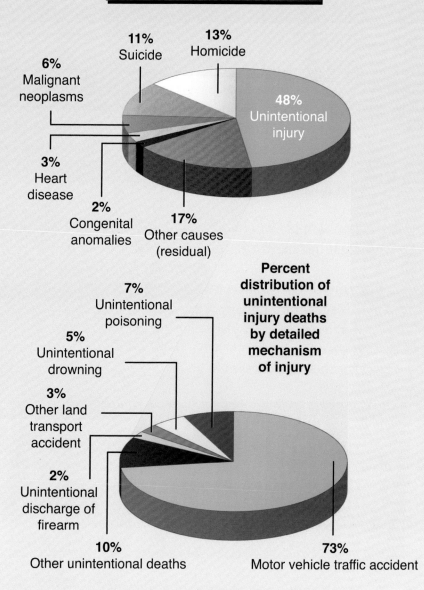

Causes of Teen Death

11% Suicide

13% Homicide

6% Malignant neoplasms

48% Unintentional injury

3% Heart disease

2% Congenital anomalies

17% Other causes (residual)

Percent distribution of unintentional injury deaths by detailed mechanism of injury

7% Unintentional poisoning

5% Unintentional drowning

3% Other land transport accident

2% Unintentional discharge of firearm

10% Other unintentional deaths

73% Motor vehicle traffic accident

Taken from: Centers for Disease Control and Prevention, National Vital Statistics System.

who was the chief scientist with the Insurance Institute for Highway Safety.

Deaths of 16-year-old drivers increased from 86 to 107 (a 24 percent change), while the number for 17-year-old drivers went from 116 to 133 (a 15 percent change), a cumulative increase of 19 percent.

Twenty-five states reported increases, 17 had decreases, and eight states and the District of Columbia reported no change in the number of 16- and 17-year-old driver deaths.

Dr. Williams attributes much of the increase to the fact that the benefit of state Graduated Driver Licensing (GDL) laws may be leveling off, as most of these laws have been in place for some time. Additionally, Dr. Williams speculates that improving economic conditions may be contributing to an increase in teen driving, thus increasing their exposure to risk. Dr. Williams notes, "Based on 2011 final data and the early look at 2012, it appears that we are headed [in] the wrong direction when it comes to deaths of 16- and 17-year-old drivers."

One has to wonder whether there's a relationship between the increase in fatalities and the decrease in school-based driver-ed training.

Dr. Williams stresses that while the news is certainly not good, deaths in this age group remain at a historically low level. He notes, "We are still at a much better place than we were ten or even five years earlier. However, the goal is to strive toward zero deaths, so our aim would be that these deaths should go down every year."

EVALUATING THE AUTHOR'S ARGUMENTS:

Viewpoint author Gregg Laskoski speculates on some of the causes for the recent surge in teen driver deaths. Do you think the author's speculations are valid? Why or why not?

Teen Driver Fatalities Have Decreased

Sam Obar

"Teen driver fatalities have fallen to a record low . . . nationwide."

In the following viewpoint Sam Obar maintains that fatalities for American teen drivers have fallen over the past few decades. Although car accidents are still the leading cause of death among youths, various new restrictions on drivers who are under the age of eighteen have helped to lower risks, the author contends. The graduated driver's license, for example, slowly allows teen drivers more privileges after they fulfill several prerequisites that give them road experience. In many states teens cannot drive with underage passengers in the car or while using cell phones. These restrictions are effective because they reduce the number of distractions for teen drivers, Obar argues. Obar is a columnist for the *Walpole Times* in Walpole, Massachusetts.

AS YOU READ, CONSIDER THE FOLLOWING QUESTIONS:

1. According to the author, how many American teens died in car accidents in 1975? How many in 2010?
2. What restrictions are placed on teens with junior operators' licenses, according to Obar?
3. Why is AAA spokesperson Mary Maguire reluctant to applaud the ban on cell phones for junior operators, according to the author?

For most teens, obtaining a drivers' license means newfound freedom and independence. For many decades, it also meant something more sobering: a higher risk than any other age group that they would die on the road.

But new statistics indicate that risk is diminishing. Teen driver fatalities have fallen to a record low in Massachusetts and nationwide.

According to the National Highway Traffic Safety Administration, the number of teen drivers who died in car accidents in Massachusetts dropped to a low of 51 in 2010, the most recent year for which data are available. That made 2010 the third straight year that teen driver fatalities fell in Massachusetts.

Across the country, only 3,115 teens were killed in 2010, a far cry from the high of more than 8,000 teens who were killed in 1975. Even at the lower number, car accidents remain the leading cause of death among teenagers.

The Graduated Drivers' License

Mary Maguire, spokeswoman for AAA [American Automobile Association] Southern New England, says the state's move to a graduated drivers' license with a new junior operators' license (JOL) in 2006 is a major reason for the drop. "The JOLs have definitely been a factor. There is no doubt about that," Maguire says.

Different versions of a graduated license system, designed to gradually grant a teen driver more privileges as he or she gains more experience on the road, have been enacted in all 50 states, starting with Florida in 1996. In Massachusetts, teens can get their learner's permit at age 16 and must take 30 hours of a driver's education course along with 40 hours of supervised driving with someone over 21. The driver's education requirement is waived if they are over 18.

After six months with a permit, teens may take a road test to obtain a junior license. Junior operators cannot drive with underage passengers in the car and cannot drive at certain hours of the night without

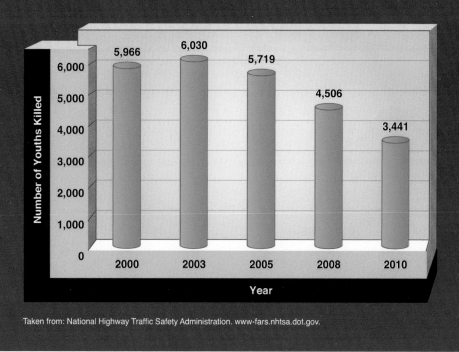

Numbers of Youths Aged Sixteen to Twenty Killed in Car Accidents, by Year

Taken from: National Highway Traffic Safety Administration. www-fars.nhtsa.dot.gov.

adult supervision. They face license suspension and/or fines if they violate the restrictions or receive a speeding ticket. The JOL restrictions are lifted when the licensee turns 18.

Diminishing Risks

"Those laws are aimed at taking teens out of the situations that research shows are the most risky—things like driving with other teen passengers in the car and driving at night," says Russ Rader, spokesman for the Insurance Institute for Highway Safety.

Peter Ellis, a 17-year-old from Walpole, is one of those affected by the JOL law. Ellis, who got his license earlier this year [2012], has so far avoided getting into an accident or even being pulled over. While he readily admits he isn't a fan of the passenger restriction or waiting so long between permit and license, he acknowledges the safety aspects. "I know that with passengers in the car, I'm probably going to crash so I just don't do that," Ellis says.

A graduated driver's license class meets in Atlantic City, New Jersey. The classes are designed to gradually grant a teen driver more privileges as he or she gains more experience on the road.

Another major component of the law is the requirement that parents attend a special class before their son or daughter can get their license. Maguire says the class—which Massachusetts is the first and, so far, only state to require—has been highly successful.

"The parent class has enlightened a lot of parents and made them aware of the need to place restrictions on their teens," Maguire says.

Cell Phone Bans

Maguire thinks the state's texting-while-driving law, passed in 2010, may also be a factor in the reduction in fatalities. The law bans all drivers from texting, but includes a total ban on junior operators from using cell phones in any manner while driving. An 18-year-old Haverhill man was found guilty in June [2012] of killing another driver while the then 17-year-old teen was texting and driving and was sentenced to a year in jail.

"You reduce the number of distractions for teens who are the most at-risk group of drivers, and that makes a difference," Maguire says.

But because teen crash statistics aren't yet available for 2011 or 2012, Maguire cautioned that it might be premature to declare the ban a success. Rader also says it's too early to tell how successful the ban actually is. A 2008 study by the Insurance Institute conducted in North Carolina found that even after a cell phone ban was enacted, teenagers actually used cell phones while driving more than they did before the ban.

Americans Are Driving Less

For Ellis and other teens, economic conditions may also be at play. Because he can't afford to buy a car and relies on his parents' cars and gas to get him where he needs to go, he isn't on the road very often. The statistics suggest he's not alone. According to the federal traffic safety administration, Americans as a whole drove 1.2 percent less in 2011 than they did in 2010—a decrease of 35.7 billion miles. The Federal Highway Administration also reported that total gasoline consumption went down by 1.9 percent between 2010 and 2011.

"I would think that the high price of gasoline has had a chilling effect on teen driving," Maguire says. "I think gas prices have led all drivers to drive less."

EVALUATING THE AUTHOR'S ARGUMENTS:

Viewpoint author Sam Obar maintains that the risks associated with teen driving have diminished because of new laws. What evidence does he provide to support his argument? Are you convinced by this evidence? Why or why not?

Viewpoint
3

Cell Phones Increase the Dangers for Teen Drivers

Randy Dotinga

"The most compulsive [teen] cellphone users have had more car accidents."

In the following viewpoint *HealthDay* reporter Randy Dotinga summarizes the findings of two studies conducted to observe the links between cell phone use and accidents among young drivers. The first study found that texting made teen drivers at least two times more likely to drift or to have near misses with cars and pedestrians. The second study concluded that compulsive cell phone users are more likely to have accidents than are those who are not compulsive cell phone users. Dotinga contends, however, that other factors—such as being easily distracted—might affect the rate of accidents among teen drivers who use cell phones.

AS YOU READ, CONSIDER THE FOLLOWING QUESTIONS:
1. According to Dotinga, what was the main purpose of the cell phone study conducted by Oklahoma high school students?
2. According to the Whitehill study, cited by the author, how many annual crashes per hundred students occur among compulsive cell phone users?
3. What should adults emphasize when trying to prevent cell phone use among teen drivers, according to Dotinga?

A pair of new studies offers insight into young people who use cellphones while driving: One finds that there's no safe position for texting at the wheel, while the other suggests that the most compulsive cellphone users have had more car accidents.

The latter study "points to a link" between driving mishaps and young people who show symptoms similar to those of addiction when it comes to cellphone use, said lead author Jennifer Whitehill, a postdoctoral researcher at the University of Washington's Harborview Injury Prevention and Research Center.

"We need to know if compulsive use of cellphones is predictive of the future" when it comes to accidents, Whitehill said. "If so, we may be able to identify these people and possibly counsel them." The studies [we]re slated for presentation [on April 29, 2012,] at the annual meeting of the Pediatric Academic Societies, in Boston.

A High School Student Study

One study was conducted by Oklahoma high school students who are taking part in a community effort to stop teen drivers and families from texting on their cellphones while driving. The study sought to answer this question: Is there a safer way to position a cellphone in order to text while driving?

Thirty participants aged 15 to 19 used driving simulators in one of three ways: without a cellphone; while texting with the phone in a position that forced them to look downward to see messages; and while texting with the phone in a position of their choice.

FAST FACT

Taking one's eyes off the road for just two seconds doubles the risk of a crash, according to the AAA Foundation for Traffic Safety.

The teen drivers were about four to six times more likely to drift out of their lanes in the simulation if they were texting, no matter where they put the phone. They were also twice as likely to have near misses with cars and pedestrians if they were texting, regardless of where the phone was.

A recent study in Oklahoma found that teen drivers were twice as likely to have near misses with cars and pedestrians if they were using a cell phone.

Compulsive Cellphone Use

In the other study, Whitehill and colleagues gave surveys to 384 undergraduate students that were designed to detect whether they were compulsive users of cellphones. Among other things, the questions asked whether they are emotionally attached to their cellphones, often anticipate calls or messages, and can't function normally due to cellphone use.

The idea was to get at whether "you are thinking about your phone even when you're not using, when it's off," she said.

The survey also asked about whether the participants had been in car accidents previously.

"The folks who scored higher on compulsive cellphone use had more prior crashes," Whitehill said.

The study estimates that "if we had a group of 100 students with the lowest scores on the (compulsive scale), we would expect that 25 had a crash in the last year," she said. "Among 100 students with the highest scores, we would see 38 crashes. That's an extra 13 crashes per 100 students within the high-risk group."

However, Whitehill said, the study doesn't prove that compulsive cellphone use directly led to more accidents. It's possible that another factor—such as being easily distracted—might account for both. "We didn't ask about other types of anxious behaviors or general difficulties with being easily distracted," she said.

Changing Dangerous Behaviors

Paul Atchley, an associate professor of psychology at the University of Kansas who studies driving and is familiar with Whitehill's findings, said: "Studies like this are critical for traffic safety professionals trying to change this dangerous behavior. We need to understand the mind of our drivers to know how to help them change these dangerous behaviors."

When it comes to preventing cellphone use while driving, adults should emphasize "the positive effects of staying off the phone while driving as opposed to the negative effects of being on it," said Jessica Mirman, a behavioral researcher at the Center for Injury Research and Prevention at The Children's Hospital of Philadelphia.

Because the studies were presented at a medical meeting, the data and conclusions should be viewed as preliminary until published in a peer-reviewed journal.

EVALUATING THE AUTHOR'S ARGUMENTS:

Citing two studies, Randy Dotinga asserts that the use of cell phones increases the rate of car accidents for teen drivers; however, one of the studies suggests that distractibility—and not solely cell phone use—may be at the root of most of these accidents. In your opinion, which is more dangerous: being easily distracted while driving or using cell phones while driving? Explain, using evidence from the viewpoints in your answer.

Viewpoint

4

Multiple Distractions Increase the Dangers for Teen Drivers

"[Thirty-eight percent] of teens have been scared while riding with a distracted driver."

Holly Corbett

Distracted driving greatly increases a teen's chances of being in a car accident, writes Holly Corbett in the following viewpoint. Texting while driving is notoriously distracting—but so is driving with too many passengers, as is eating or changing radio stations while driving, the author points out. She shares the stories of several youths whose lives were impacted by distracted driving and offers suggestions on how teens can increase their safety while driving and while riding with others. Corbett, coauthor of *The Lost Girls,* is a writer and editor based in New York City.

AS YOU READ, CONSIDER THE FOLLOWING QUESTIONS:

1. How many people die each year due to distracted driving, according to the author?
2. As Corbett explains, texting while driving is as dangerous as driving after drinking how many beers?
3. How might a driver make it easier to ignore his or her cell phone, in the author's view?

You've heard plenty of stories about how distracted driving is dangerous and how it's the cause of scary crashes. But with all the stuff you have going on, it's easy to justify sending that quick text or calling to report you're running late. Sometimes you've got downtime while you're driving, so you start thinking about something you forgot to tell your best friend—and it feels like it absolutely can't wait. You know it's bad, but then you think, What is the harm in looking down for a split second to send a message? But the thing is, the nearly 6,000 people who die every year from distracted driving thought the same thing. Check out these stories of girls . . . whose lives have changed forever because of a few seconds of distracted driving, and find out what you need to know to keep it from ever happening to you!

Texting is just one of the dangers teens engage in while driving. Others include joyriding with friends, eating while driving, and looking for or changing a radio station, CD, or selections on an MP3 player.

Things Drivers Do That Take Their Eyes and Focus off the Road

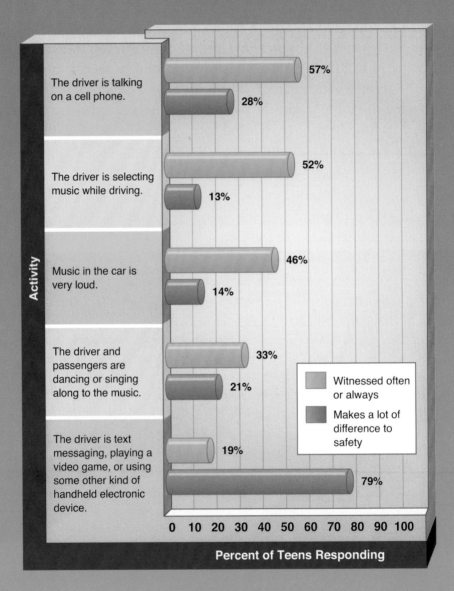

The driver is talking on a cell phone. — 57% / 28%

The driver is selecting music while driving. — 52% / 13%

Music in the car is very loud. — 46% / 14%

The driver and passengers are dancing or singing along to the music. — 33% / 21%

The driver is text messaging, playing a video game, or using some other kind of handheld electronic device. — 19% / 79%

Activity

Witnessed often or always

Makes a lot of difference to safety

0 10 20 30 40 50 60 70 80 90 100

Percent of Teens Responding

Taken from: F.K. Winston, et al., eds. *Driving Through the Eyes of Teens, A Closer Look.* Children's Hospital of Philadelphia and State Farm Insurance Companies®, 2009.

Cheyenne's Story: "A Text Message Almost Killed Me!"

It was like any other Monday night when my friend Rahela and I were driving to her cousin's house, rocking out to the radio. She took her eyes off the road for a second to show me a text, or I was showing her something on my phone—I can't remember which. All of a sudden, she swerved and we crossed into the other lane into oncoming traffic. I screamed her name before we hit an SUV and then everything went black. The next thing I knew, I was waking up with a paramedic standing over me and heard Rahela crying. I wasn't in pain, just totally numb. I thought I was sweating, so I wiped my face—my hands were red with blood. I started to cry too. I was so scared.

When we got to the hospital, my grandmother was there and she kept saying how happy she was that I was alive. She stayed with me while the doctors pulled glass from the windshield out of my eye. I broke my left leg, nose, a couple of ribs, and even bit through my tongue where my tongue ring was. I had to get staples in my leg to stitch up an almost 10-inch-long gash. For the next two months, I walked with crutches and endured painful physical therapy. The doctors thought Rahela was going to have permanent brain damage since her head smashed so hard into the steering wheel, but she was lucky to escape with just a con-

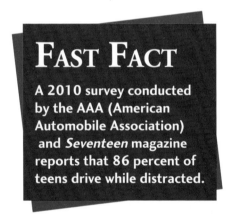

FAST FACT

A 2010 survey conducted by the AAA (American Automobile Association) and *Seventeen* magazine reports that 86 percent of teens drive while distracted.

cussion and a battered face. Whenever I look in the mirror or see a picture of myself, I'm reminded of the crash because of the scars on my face. I understand why people want to keep their phones on in the car. But if it's sitting in your lap going off, you're going to want to check it. What's more important—text or your life?—Cheyenne, 18, Lincoln, NB

Sneaky Car Crimes

You know texting and driving isn't safe, but these under-the-radar moves are just as dangerous!

- *Turning your car into a taxi.* When everyone is piled in and trading stories, you can't possibly focus on the road. Draw the line at three friends—max.

- *Doing the drive-through.* Eating in the car means your focus is on dipping sauce, not traffic. Pulling into a parking space to scarf your Big Mac could prevent a crash.
- *Station-surfing.* Commercials and sappy songs are annoying, but fiddling with your radio makes you take your eyes off the road. Plug in a playlist of your favorite songs before you turn on the ignition.

Amber's Mission

Amber, 22, lost her best friend, Casey, when she was killed in a crosswalk by a driver who glanced away from the road. That day, Amber vowed that no one else would ever die from something so preventable. So last spring [2009], Amber and her honors fraternity organized a local benefit concert. To promote it, they stood at an intersection on campus where two other girls had been hit, and waved signs that said, "Honk for Safe Driving." They sold T-shirts to help raise $2,600 for charities like The Partnership for Safe Driving, which educates people about all kinds of dangerous driving. To spread the word or organize your own event, go to caseyfeldmannetwork.org.

DWT: Driving While Texting

You wouldn't drive drunk, right? Well, texting and driving can be as dangerous as chugging four beers and getting behind the wheel, and it makes you 23 times more likely to get into an accident!

PS: Make it easy to ignore your phone. Go to getizup.com to download an app to your smart phone that automatically sends any incoming calls straight to your voicemail while your car is in motion and holds texts until you've pulled over.

Avoid a Car-Tastrophe

In a dangerous situation? Here's how to defuse it.

The situation: Your friend keeps texting while she's driving.

You say: "Hey, can I borrow your phone to make a call? My cell service is spotty."

The situation: Your friends all want to cram into your car.

You say: "I can only take three—my parents will take away my car if they know it's packed, and we can't be sneaky with all these people!"

The situation: Your friend always pays more attention to the radio than to the road.

You say: "I made you a song list. Let me play this new tune for you." Or just be direct, "Dude, you're going to kill us both. Quit it!"

38% of teens have been scared while riding with a distracted driver.

EVALUATING THE AUTHOR'S ARGUMENTS:

At the end of this viewpoint, Holly Corbett offers several suggestions on how teens—both passengers and drivers—can help each other avoid distracted driving. Do you think that these suggestions will work? Why or why not?

Passengers Increase the Chance of Accidents for Teen Drivers

*"[Teens']
risk of a
fatal crash
multiplies
when they
have other
teenagers in
the car."*

Ashley Halsey III

The more young passengers a car contains, the more likely a teen driver is to have an accident, reports Ashley Halsey III in the following selection. This particular fatality statistic lends support to the argument that parents should refuse to allow their children to ride in cars driven by unsupervised teens, the author reasons. Accordingly, most states now limit the number of nonfamily passengers who can be in a car with teen drivers. Halsey is a staff reporter for the *Washington Post.*

AS YOU READ, CONSIDER THE FOLLOWING QUESTIONS:

1. How often do teenagers crash compared with older drivers, according to the author?
2. When a teenage driver has three passengers in the car, the risk of a fatal crash increases by how much, according to Halsey?
3. According to a study conducted by the National Highway Traffic Safety Administration and cited by Halsey, which age group is most likely to send and receive text messages while driving?

Last month, [April 2012] it was four teenagers in a stolen Toyota who crashed into a Montgomery County [Maryland] tree. Three of them—two were 16, the other 14—died.

In January, it was three teens on their way home from a birthday party who headed in the wrong direction on a divided highway in Anne Arundel County [Maryland] in the middle of the night, colliding head-on with another car. Everyone died.

The Most Dangerous Drivers

For generations, teenagers have been the most dangerous drivers on the road, crashing almost four times as often as older drivers. A study released Tuesday [May 8, 2012,] quantifies, for the first time in a decade, how their risk of a fatal crash multiplies when they have other teenagers in the car.

It increases by almost half when a 16- or 17-year-old driver has one teenage passenger; it doubles with two teen passengers; and it quadruples with three or more.

The more young passengers a teen-driven car contains, the more likely the driver is to have an accident.

Last year [2011], it was five teenagers in a car that hit a deer and then a tree in Prince William County [Maryland]. Two 15-year-olds were killed. In 2008, a Volvo carrying five teenagers to a Burger King in Montgomery County veered off a winding road and burst into flames after hitting a tree. A 15-year-old passenger died.

"He's a newer driver," said the mother of the teenager who was behind the wheel, who survived. "He just miscalculated."

A Preventable Risk

Using federal fatality statistics, AAA's [the American Automobile Association's] Foundation for Traffic Safety provided the data that will support parents who have forbidden their teenage children to drive with other teenagers.

"We know that carrying young passengers is a huge risk, but it's also a preventable one," said AAA Foundation President Peter Kissinger. "These findings should send a clear message to families that parents can make their teens safer immediately by refusing to allow them to get in the car with other young people, whether they're behind the wheel or in the passenger seat."

FAST FACT

Three passengers in the car of a teen driver increase the risk of a crash by 200 percent, according to the New Jersey Teen Safe Driving Coalition.

The AAA study is the latest of three recent reports to raise concerns about teenage drivers. In reviewing preliminary data from the first six months of last year, the Governors Highway Safety Association found a slight increase in the number of fatal crashes involving 16- and 17-year-old drivers. If the trend continued, it said, 2011 would reverse a recent trend of falling teenage fatalities.

In another study, the National Highway Traffic Safety Administration [NHTSA] last month said its research found that drivers under the age of 24 were much more likely than more mature drivers to send and receive text messages while driving.

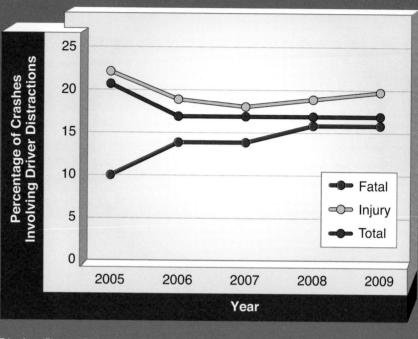

Crashes Involving Driver Distraction, by Crash Severity

Taken from: "Distracted Driving 2009." US Department of Transportation Traffic Safety Facts: Research Note, September 2010.

A Decline in Fatalities

Overall, highway fatalities fell for the sixth consecutive year in 2011, according to preliminary data NHTSA released Monday. The federal agency said that 32,310 people died in crashes last year, down 375 deaths from 2010. NHTSA will break down the statistics by age group when final data are released later this year.

If the decline in teen fatalities flattens or reverses when that information is released, it might be that the effect of state laws implemented in the past 15 years played out. Graduated licensing laws and requirements for driver education or parental supervision have been mandated in many jurisdictions, including Virginia, Maryland and the District [of Columbia].

"Placing appropriate limits is a key part of graduated driver licensing in the District of Columbia, Virginia and Maryland," said John B.

Townsend II of AAA Mid-Atlantic. "It's critical that parents enforce the law and family rules."

In addition, most states have limited the number of non-family passengers who can be carried by teen drivers.

EVALUATING THE AUTHOR'S ARGUMENTS:

Ashley Halsey III opens his essay with a few anecdotes about serious car accidents that killed several teenagers. In your opinion, how effective are these anecdotes in persuading a reader about the dangers of youths driving or riding along with others their age? Explain your answer.

Distracted Driving Puts Young Drivers at Risk

Consumer Reports

"Having peers in the car may help curb distracted driving."

In the following viewpoint Consumer Reports shares the findings of its national survey of sixteen- to twenty-one-year-old drivers. A significant percentage of youths reported that they had talked on a hand-held phone or had texted within the previous month. At the same time, however, a majority of respondents believe that texting or talking on a cell phone while driving is dangerous—with nearly 50 percent admitting that they were less likely to use a phone while driving if friends were in the car. Thus, teen drivers who have friends as passengers may be less prone to cell phone–related distracted driving. Consumer Reports is an independent nonprofit organization with the goal of promoting a fair and just marketplace and to empower consumers to protect themselves.

AS YOU READ, CONSIDER THE FOLLOWING QUESTIONS:

1. What percentage of respondents to the Consumer Reports survey, as reported by the author, admitted to using a cell phone while driving during the past thirty days?
2. According to Consumer Reports, what percentage of teen drivers who died in crashes in 2010 were distracted?
3. How many survey respondents claimed that they had asked someone to stop using a phone while driving, according to the author?

I t's dangerous to use a cell phone behind the wheel. But many teenagers and other young drivers still play the odds by talking or texting on a handheld cell phone or operating a mobile device while driving. Those are the findings of a recent nationally representative survey of drivers 16 to 21 years old by the Consumer Reports National Research Center.

FAST FACT

According to the *New England Journal of Medicine*, crash risk is four times higher when a driver uses a cell phone, whether or not it is a hands-free one.

Almost half of the respondents said they had talked on a handheld phone while driving in the previous 30 days. Close to 30 percent said they had texted in that time. And some had operated smart-phone apps (8 percent) or used e-mail or social media (7 percent) while behind the wheel.

Yet almost all of them considered texting, using smart-phone apps, or accessing the Internet to be dangerous while driving; about 80 percent thought it was very dangerous. Also, 63 percent of those surveyed saw talking on a handheld phone while driving as dangerous.

Moreover, most respondents had seen their peers doing similar things in that time. Eighty-four percent saw other young people talking on a handheld phone, more than 70 percent witnessed texting, and about a third saw peers using apps, e-mail, or social media behind the wheel.

Why is that dangerous? Motor-vehicle crashes are the No. 1 cause of death for teenagers, according to the National Highway Traffic Safety Administration. And 11 percent of teenage drivers who died in crashes in 2010 were distracted. Our survey results indicate that young drivers are engaging in behavior that causes them to take their eyes and minds off the road, creating risks for themselves and others.

Young drivers were also asked about the driving habits of Mom and Dad. Forty-eight percent witnessed their parents talking on a handheld phone in the previous 30 days, and 15 percent saw them texting.

What's Working

Concern about distracted driving led almost three-quarters of those surveyed to stop or reduce such behavior, they said. More than 60 percent said they were influenced by reading or hearing about the problem, 40 percent by related bans, and close to 30 percent by their family urging them to stop. Almost 20 percent knew someone who had been in a crash caused by distracted driving.

Our survey also found that having peers in the car may help curb distracted driving. Almost 50 percent said they were less likely to talk on a handheld cell phone or text when friends were along. One reason may be that many young people are speaking up; almost half

Top Causes of Distracted Driving

1. Cell phone use
2. Reaching for a moving object inside the vehicle
3. Looking at an object or event outside the window
4. Reading
5. Applying makeup

Taken from: California Department of Motor Vehicles. "Driver Distractions—Don't Be a Statistic," 2011.

In a recent survey, almost 50 percent of teen drivers said they were less likely to talk on the phone or text when friends were riding with them.

said they had asked a driver to stop using a phone in the car because they feared for their safety.

Whether you're a parent, friend, or sibling, set a good example. Stop the car in a safe place if you need to use a cell phone. And if you're riding with a driver using a phone, ask him or her to put it down and stop gambling with your safety.

Sending the Wrong Message to Future Drivers

The temptation to mix cell phones with driving may be starting earlier than we thought. A number of children's "driving" toys—including play cars, trikes, and toy steering wheels—now include toy cell phones as part of the package.

We're not aware of injuries resulting from children multitasking with toy vehicles, but including toy cell phones sends an early message that the behavior is acceptable.

Tom McClure, marketing director at VTech Electronics, which sells the 3-in-1 Smart Wheels above, told us, "We have not seen the opinions you express cited in any studies, but we will certainly continue to make sure we are informed of any issues affecting children's development."

To teach children about the risks of distracted driving, parents need to educate them years before they hand over the real keys. We hope toy makers will support the government and safety advocates in promoting safe driving by disassociating toy vehicles and phones in their products.

EVALUATING THE AUTHOR'S ARGUMENTS:

In this viewpoint's final paragraphs, the author, Consumer Reports, discusses children's driving toys, many of which include toy cell phones as part of the package. Consumer Reports believes that it is important to teach children about the risks of distracted driving, and that one way of doing that would be to stop including toy cell phones in toy vehicle sets. Do you agree or disagree with this tactic? Explain your answer.

Chapter 2

Are Current Laws for Teen Drivers Appropriate?

Connecticut governor M. Jodi Rell signs a bill tightening teen driving laws in 2008. Many states have passed bills restricting teen driving.

Viewpoint 1

The Driving Age Should Be Raised

"Teenagers, the people we should be protecting, are four times as likely to die in a road accident than as a result of drink or drugs."

Joanna Moorhead

The minimum age for driving should be raised, argues Joanna Moorhead in the following viewpoint. In her opinion, licensing drivers in their teens is dangerous because youths at that age are immature and much more likely to underestimate the hazards of the road. They may take not only their lives, but the lives of those in the car or on the road. The author believes it is up to the law to protect immature drivers by increasing the driving age requirements. Moorhead writes for the *Guardian*, a newspaper in Manchester, England, focusing mainly on parenting and family life.

AS YOU READ, CONSIDER THE FOLLOWING QUESTIONS:

1. In the opinion of the Transport Research Laboratory, what age should youths be before they start learning to drive, according to the author?
2. According the Moorhead, what personal tragedy did her family experience that impacted her feelings toward teenage drivers?
3. Beyond raising the driving age, what other limitation on teen driving would keep drivers safer, according to a government report cited by Moorhead?

Would you give a child a loaded gun? Loaded guns are unbelievably dangerous, and children's brains not yet capable of properly understanding danger, or heeding warnings. Of course you wouldn't.

But would you allow a 17-year-old to drive a car? We've all been right behind it, for many years: or at least, no one I know has been out on the streets protesting about the threshold at which teenagers can apply for a provisional driving licence.

But now, at last, sanity is starting to prevail. A government report [in the United Kingdom], by the Transport Research Laboratory, has recommended raising the age at which kids can learn to drive to 18. My 15-year-old daughter, who is counting the months until she's almost 17 (the application can go in three months before their birthday) will be devastated when she hears the news—and so will thousands of other teens, for whom getting a licence and learning to drive is seen as a rite of passage.

But I use the word "kids" deliberately. Anyone who has older children—and I have two, aged 21 and 19—knows they are really toddlers in an extraordinarily effective disguise. They look (especially if you don't currently have one) so adult! All grown-up! But—and there's an increasing amount of research to back this up—until they're at least 21, their brains are still in formation. They don't yet "think" like adults; in particular, they don't connect "actions" and "consequences". If you're a driver, you know how bad that could be.

And yet we give them the car keys; we sit beside them as they learn the difference between the accelerator and the brake; we applaud when they pass their driving test; we pay the extortionate insurance premiums for them. And still we don't twig [understand] how bonkers it all is: unless your family is hit by tragedy when a teenager crashes, and suddenly it's all crystal clear. My husband's cousin crashed, fresh from her driving test. She survived for two years in a coma, but then she died. A young woman who would

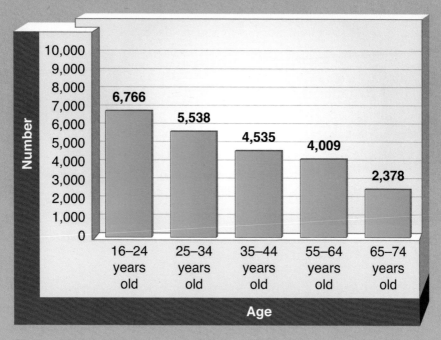

Persons Killed in Car Accidents in 2010, by Age

Number

10,000				
9,000				
8,000				
7,000	**6,766**			
6,000		**5,538**		
5,000			**4,535**	
4,000				**4,009**
3,000				**2,378**
2,000				
1,000				
0	16–24 years old	25–34 years old	35–44 years old	55–64 years old	65–74 years old

Age

Taken from: National Highway Traffic Safety Administration. www-fars.nhtsa.dot.gov.

now be in her mid-30s, carried off way too soon, more by society's negligence than by her inexperience as a driver.

And when it happens: wham. Not just the impact—which is immeasurable, because road traffic deaths blight families for decades after people assume they're "over it"—but the madness of it all. Why did that child have a loaded gun?

Sometimes it's not only themselves they kill either: they take their siblings, their friends, with them.

Once you've been hit by a road traffic death—and my family has, as well as my husband's—you know its impossible to overestimate its toll. And the terrible reality is that road deaths are the most common tragedy in all our lives; and teenagers, the people we should be protecting, are four times as likely to die in a road accident than as a result of drink or drugs. Four times! And here's betting you've heard far more about the dangers of drink and drugs.

More than five thousand teenagers die and more than three hundred thousand are injured each year in traffic accidents.

Today's [October 11, 2013] government report urges more than just rowing back on the age threshold. It suggests a lot of hand-holding, as you would do for a young child. A night-time curfew, unless they have an over-30 with them (what a delightful idea that is—my taxi beckons, after all those years when it's been the other way round), and a learner phase when they drive under supervision.

Some people will call it the nanny state. But I bet you this: none of them are people who've ever watched a teenage driver's coffin being lowered into the earth. It's not a sight you easily forget; and nor should it be.

EVALUATING THE AUTHOR'S ARGUMENTS:

Joanna Moorhead cites her own personal story of family tragedy as evidence that the teenage driving age should be increased. Does her personal narrative provide good support for her argument that the driving age should be raised? Why or why not?

The Driving Age Should Not Be Raised

Eric Peters

"[A driver's] experience and training probably mean a whole lot more than age."

In the viewpoint that follows Eric Peters argues against raising the minimum driving age to eighteen. In his view the high rate of car accidents among US teens is due to their lack of experience and poor training, not their age. A better plan would be to lower the age at which youths start learning to drive and to offer them high-quality driver's education with expert instructors who build their skills up gradually, the author maintains. Peters is an automotive columnist for the National Motorists Association, an organization that advocates for the rights of drivers.

AS YOU READ, CONSIDER THE FOLLOWING QUESTIONS:

1. At what age should teenagers start learning to drive, in the author's opinion?
2. What institutions are to blame for the lower quality of driver's education, in Peters's view?
3. According to Peters, what is the problem with relying on parents to teach their children how to drive?

Is 16 too young to drive?

If you're 16, you probably think not. But it's those over 16—adults like the Insurance Institute for Highway Safety's [IIHS's] Adrian Lund—who will get to be the deciders on this one. Lund and some others want to push the age at which a person can get their first driver's license to 17 or even 18.

Of course, it's all about "safety."

Lund—professional nag who heads an organization of nags—says that teenage drivers are a menace to themselves and others and wants to use the billy stick of the federal government (via withheld highway funds) to compel states to raise their legal driving age—just as the billy stick of federal money was used to impose the 55 mph speed limit, virtual Prohibition of alcohol and "primary enforcement" [of] seat belt laws.

This time, it's not merely "for the children"—it actually involves them.

Age Versus Experience

And Lund is partially right. Teenagers do get into more than their fair share of wrecks. But is this due to their age—or their lack of training/experience?

There are some very young pro drivers—from NHRA [National Hot Rod Association] to NASCAR [National Association for Stock Car Auto Racing]. Maybe not sixteen-year-olds, but not far removed. At 15 or 16, some of these kids are better drivers than most of us will ever be. What to make of this fact?

Granted, these are exceptional kids—but the point's not invalid: Experience and training probably mean a whole lot more than age—as such.

Will raising the age to 17 or 18 give a kid more experience—or less? Maybe the age at which we begin to train kids to drive should be lowered, not raised. Does it make more—or less—sense to toss a kid with zero hours behind the wheel a set of car keys at 17 or 18, when he is inches way from being legally free of any parental oversight whatsoever?

FAST FACT

The greatest lifetime chance of crashing occurs in the first six months after licensure, according to researchers.

Driver's Education Does Not Improve Teen Driving Skills

Nearly 5 percent of 51,000 teens who took driver's education had one or more reported accidents, compared with 1 percent of 71,932 drivers without formal education.

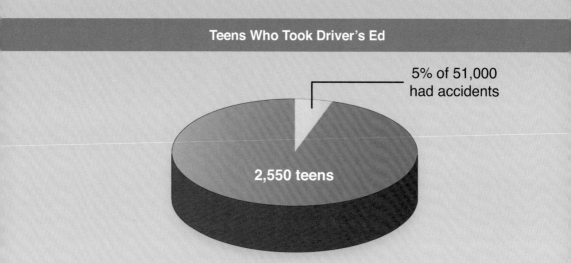

Teens Who Took Driver's Ed

5% of 51,000 had accidents

2,550 teens

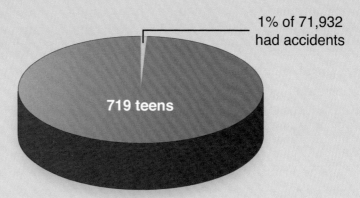

Teens Who Did Not Take Driver's Ed

1% of 71,932 had accidents

719 teens

Taken from: Stephen J. Dubner. "Does Driver's Ed Lead to More Car Crashes?" September 8, 2010. www.freakonomics.com.

Maybe it would make more sense to begin teaching kids how to drive around 14 or 15—easing them into it gradually, and with supervision—so that by the time they are 17 or 18 they have three or four years of experience behind them. That's actually the way it used to be done, until public institutions such as public schools took over from parents and the whole process became bureaucratized and officialized—but with less than stellar results.

What Makes More Sense?

Driving is, after all, a skill like any other; it is not mastered overnight—or after a few weeks of classroom instruction and a couple of hours in the seat.

Logic says start them sooner, not later.

But that would make sense—and making sense is what IIHS is not all about. It exists to harp over problems often directly ginned up by its own propaganda. Mandatory buckle-up laws are an example of this. Ditto the neo-Prohibitionist crusade that has gone way beyond a legitimate effort to deal with drunk drivers that now mercilessly prosecutes people with trace amounts of alcohol in their system—as little as .06 or even .04 BAC [blood alcohol concentration], the level an average person can reach after having had a single glass of wine over dinner.

But I digress.

Proper Instruction

The other half of the equation when it comes to new/teenage drivers is proper instruction. What we do in this country—for the most part—is woefully inadequate. Many parents set poor examples—or are simply ill-equipped to properly instruct their kids in safe/competent driving. Ditto the so-called "schools" (especially those offered by the public schools) and the at-best cursory testing done by most DMVs [Departments of Motor Vehicles] before that first license is issued.

We don't really show kids how to drive—especially how to handle [an] emergency, such as a slide on black ice. Instead, we chant cant at them that's obvious BS, such as "speed kills"—the driving equivalent of the BS about "marihuana" that's peddled to them in Just Say No

Proper instruction from a qualified instructor is perhaps the most important part of learning to drive. Most parents are ill-equipped to instruct their children in proper driving techniques.

sessions. Kids are smart enough to see through this—but immature enough to then regard everything they're taught by adults as BS.

This is dangerous.

Far better to really teach them—and to be honest with them.

I'd be ready to lay serious cash on the table to bet Lund that if you took an average 14 or 15 year old and had him or her trained by an expert instructor and properly supervised for a year or two before a provisional license was granted—after which the kid would still be monitored and quickly reined in at the first sign of reckless or incompetent behavior—the whole "teenage driver" thing would just disappear.

Problem is, there's no money in that. Finding solutions to problems is not what IIHS wants. IIHS wants crusades that never end. Just like MADD [Mothers Against Drunk Driving]; just like politicians. Just like the whole lot of them.

EVALUATING THE AUTHOR'S ARGUMENTS:

How would you describe the tone of Eric Peters's viewpoint? In your opinion, does this tone enhance his argument or detract from it? Explain your answer.

Graduated Driver's Licenses: Opinions, Policies Vary

Alesha Williams Boyd

"All 50 states have, since the 1990s, put in place three graduated licensing stages."

In the following viewpoint Alesha Williams Boyd examines some of the different state graduated driver's license requirements. The graduated driver's license usually progresses through three stages—a minimum supervised learner's period, an intermediate license that limits unsupervised driving in high-risk situations, and, lastly, a full-privilege driver's license. The restrictions at each stage vary by state. Boyd reports for *USA Today* and for the *Ashbury Park (NJ) Press*.

AS YOU READ, CONSIDER THE FOLLOWING QUESTIONS:

1. According to the author, what was the increase in the number of teen drivers and passengers killed in traffic accidents in 2011 in the state of New Jersey?
2. How many hours of supervised driving does Oregon require, according to the author?
3. In Kansas unsupervised intermediate drivers must be off the road by what time, according to the author?

B y the end of her driver's lesson with a Skillful Driving School instructor outside her family's home here, 16-year-old Samantha Miller had executed about a dozen K-turns and parallel-parked another dozen times.

She knew she would do it all over again at her next lesson. And that was OK with Samantha.

In New Jersey, the number of teen drivers and passengers killed in traffic accidents in 2011 increased to a total of 50, up from 33 deaths the year before, according to a state police analysis. She doesn't want to be next.

"It scares me to the point where I want to make sure I'm good before I go out and try things," Samantha said. "I just want to be a good driver."

To that end, all 50 states have, since the 1990s, put in place three graduated licensing stages—a minimum supervised learner's period, an intermediate license that limits unsupervised driving in high-risk situations, and, lastly, a full-privilege driver's license.

The stages come with varying degrees of regulations depending on which state you're in:

- Oregon requires 100 hours of supervised driving, more than any other state, or 50 hours and a state-approved traffic-safety education course, while South Dakota has no specific minimum for supervised driving hours.
- Teens in Alaska, Arkansas, Iowa, Kansas and North and South Dakota are allowed on the road as young as 14 as learners; in states including Massachusetts, New York, Pennsylvania and Rhode Island, not until age 16.
- In Indiana and Maine, unsupervised intermediate drivers can't give their friends a ride for the first six months, while Iowa and Florida have no passenger restrictions.
- In Kansas, unsupervised intermediate drivers must be off the road at 9 PM, the earliest restriction; in Rhode Island, not until

1 AM Vermont is the only state without a nighttime driving restriction.

- The use of cellphones by novice drivers is restricted in 30 states and the District of Columbia, according to the Insurance Institute for Highway Safety. And 45 states and D.C. restrict the number of passengers during the intermediate stage, according to the Governors Highway Safety Association.

Not everyone agrees that these restrictions make for better teen drivers.

In New Jersey, where a red decal became required in 2010 on the license plates of drivers under 21 without full privileges, some were concerned about profiling by police and the potential to tip off stalkers.

New Jersey is the only state with a decal requirement.

"All it does is stigmatize young drivers, whether they're good or bad," says Bill Bystricky, campaign director for the Washington, D.C.–based National Youth Rights Association, which opposed the measure. "If you're going to do something like this, stigmatize bad drivers of all ages, not just young drivers including the good ones."

Public hearings were conducted by the North Dakota Senate Transportation Committee about proposed legislation to impose greater restrictions on the state's teenage drivers.

After several fatal crashes involving teens in North Carolina, the Legislature introduced a bill last year that would have required 120 hours of practice driving with a parent, more than any state in the U.S.; that number was subsequently cut down to 60 hours and passed into law.

"For the state to say thou shalt do 40, 50, 60 hours is pretty much irrelevant because most parents are doing it anyway," says Rob Foss, senior research scientist and director of the Center for the Study of Young Drivers at the University of North Carolina Highway Safety Research Center.

Foss says that, in some cases, heavier penalties such as suspensions for young drivers serve only to "delay (teens') licenses and give them no chance to learn."

And even at 18 and up, in states where older teens are allowed to skip graduated licensing requirements, they're technically still new and more prone to accidents, says Pam Fischer of the New Jersey Teen Safe Driving Coalition. Fischer is a staunch advocate of graduated licensing regulations.

"Graduated driver licensing really does work," Fischer says. "The data's there."

Samantha, the young driver, said she wouldn't mind stricter requirements if it means saving her own and others' lives. She said she expects to have a probationary license as soon as she turns 17 in November.

"I'd be OK with (the proposed practice regulations)," she said. "It helps you get more time behind the wheel, and better at it, with more confidence."

EVALUATING THE AUTHOR'S ARGUMENTS:

The author, Alesha Williams Boyd, notes some of the graduated driver's license requirements unique to particular states. Do you agree with some of the stricter teenage driving requirements? Do you think that each state should be able to create their own graduated driver's license requirements? Why or why not?

The Graduated Driver's License Does Not Protect Older Teen Drivers

"Graduated" driver license (GDL) laws do seem to curb fewer fatal crashes among 16-year-olds but not among 18-year-olds."

David W. Freeman

This viewpoint, written by David W. Freeman, questions the effectiveness of graduated driver's license programs. Although many studies show that these programs reduce accident fatalities among sixteen-year-olds, evidence also reveals an increase in fatal accidents among older teen drivers. This is likely because graduated licensing laws typically apply only to teens *younger* than eighteen, the author explains. Some teenagers are waiting until they turn eighteen to obtain a license so that they do not have to take drivers' training courses. Stronger licensing laws are needed to prevent tragic fatalities among older teen driver's, the author concludes. Freeman writes for *CBS News.*

AS YOU READ, CONSIDER THE FOLLOWING QUESTIONS:

1. Why do "graduated" driver's licensing (GDL) laws seem to curb fewer fatal crashes among 16-year-olds but not among 18-year-olds, according to the author?
2. In the author's opinion, what restrictions does New Jersey apply to all first-time applicants under age 21 that have led to lowered crash rates?
3. According the 1986–2007 study cited by the author, how many fatal crashes of drivers aged 16 to 19 were there?

D o stringent driver's license laws help keep teen motorists safe? A nationwide study shows that so-called "graduated" driver license (GDL) laws do seem to curb fewer fatal crashes among 16-year-olds but not among 18-year-olds.

Many states now require young drivers to get experience behind the wheel, including driving with an adult, before getting a license with full privileges. But those laws typically apply only to those under age 18. The new study suggests teens simply put off getting a license until they turn 18—meaning they have little experience and higher odds for a deadly crash.

"There's an incentive right now to skip out and just wait until you're 18," said study author Scott Masten, a researcher with California's Department of Motor Vehicles. "In most states you don't even need to have driver education or driver training" if you obtain a license at 18," he said, adding that the finding was disappointing and "quite unexpected."

FAST FACT

By 2012 every state in the United States had adopted the graduated driver's license.

The study—published in Wednesday's Journal of the American Medical Association— looked at fatal crashes from 1986 to 2007 involving 16- to 19-year-olds, based on data from the National Highway Traffic Safety Administration.

An editorial by researchers with the Insurance Institute for Highway Safety accompanied the study. It called the potential effects in older teens "a serious issue deserving attention by researchers and policy-makers." The editorial noted that New Jersey is one of the few states where graduated driver's licensing restrictions apply to all first-time applicants under age 21. That has led to lower crash rates among 17- and 18-year-olds.

Every state has some type of graduated driver's licensing program. These typically allow unrestricted licenses to kids under 18 only after several months of learning while driving with an adult, followed by unsupervised driving with limits on night driving and the number of passengers.

Comparing states with the most restrictions versus those with the weakest laws, there were 26 percent fewer fatal crashes involving 16-year-old drivers. But among 18-year-old drivers, there were 12 percent more fatal crashes. The differences take into account factors that would also influence fatal crash rates, including seatbelt laws,

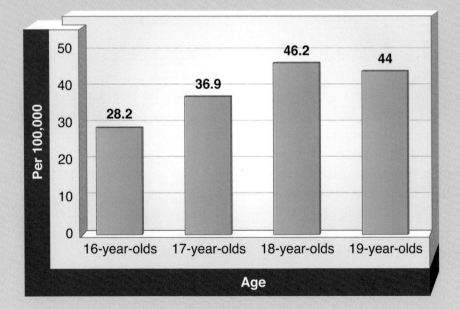

Fatal Crash Incidence Among Sixteen- to Nineteen-Year-Olds, 1986–2007

Taken from: Scott Masten et al. "Graduated Driver Licensing and Fatal Crashes Involving 16- to 19-Year-Old Drivers." *Journal of the American Medical Association*, September 14, 2011.

In Tennessee applicants under the age of eighteen applying for a driver's license must meet tough standards, such as certifying a minimum number of hours spent driving at night and at least fifty hours behind the wheel.

changes in minimum speed limits, and the fact that 18-year-old drivers outnumber 16-year-old drivers.

The programs appeared to have no effect on fatal crash rates for drivers age 17 and 19.

The first graduated licensing program began in 1996. Since then, the programs have been associated with 1,348 fewer fatal crashes involving 16-year-old drivers but with 1,086 more fatal crashes involving 18-year-old drivers.

During the 1986–2007 study, there were nearly 132,000 fatal crashes of drivers aged 16 to 19. Nearly 20 percent involved 16-year-old drivers, while almost 30 percent involved 18-year-olds.

The study confirms that graduated licensing "is doing what it was intended to do—prevent novice drivers from being in high-risk conditions before they're ready for it," said Dr. Flaura Winston, a pediatrician and traffic injury expert at the Children's Hospital of Philadelphia. But the results also demonstrate a need for strategies for the novice independent driver at any age, she said.

EVALUATING THE AUTHOR'S ARGUMENTS:

Given what you have read in this viewpoint by David W. Freeman and throughout this volume, do you think that the United States needs stronger graduated driver's licensing restrictions for older teen drivers? Explain your answer using evidence from the text.

Cars Driven by Teens Should Be Marked with Decals

Frederick L. Gruel

"The new decals will be a great tool to keeping our roads and teens safer."

In May 2011 the state of New Jersey enacted a law requiring decals on cars driven by provisional-license holders under the age of twenty-one. These decals are intended to help police officers enforce teen driving restrictions. In the following viewpoint Frederick L. Gruel argues that the decals are an improvement to current licensing laws and will make roads safer for all drivers. Without the decals, it is harder for an officer to identify which drivers are subject to the restrictions placed on teens, Gruel explains. The decals are simply a safety measure and a tool to help enforce the law, he asserts. Gruel is the president and CEO of AAA New Jersey.

AS YOU READ, CONSIDER THE FOLLOWING QUESTIONS:
  1. Where are the decals indicating a car driven by a young driver displayed, according to the author?
  2. According to Gruel, when are cars marked with decals pulled over by police?
  3. Which young drivers need not be concerned about the decals, in the author's view?

There has been much discussion surrounding the implementation of Kyleigh's law. Sadly much of this discussion has focused on misinformation and confusion—not the hard facts that led to unanimous bipartisan passage of the law in the [New Jersey] Assembly last year [2009].

The recent improvements to the Graduated Driver License (GDL), stemmed from recommendations made by New Jersey's Teen Driver Study Commission. The Commission spent nearly a year examining teen driver safety in the state, listening to parents, teens, police, prosecutors, researchers and others. Kyleigh's law was a recommendation aimed at addressing a key challenge for law enforcement. This provision went into effect just days ago [in May 2011], yet is already under attack. This enhancement to the GDL law should be given time to show its benefits.

> **FAST FACT**
>
> Kyleigh's Law is named for Kyleigh D'Alessio, a sixteen-year-old New Jersey high school student who died in a 2006 car accident while riding home with a friend.

A Successful Program

Kyleigh's law is modeled after successful programs across the globe. It enables police officers to enforce teen driving restrictions without risk of profiling drivers based on age. The removable decals, which were designed to be non-descript but easily identifiable by law enforcement, must be displayed on the front and back license plates of vehicles driven by permit or probationary license holders under 21.

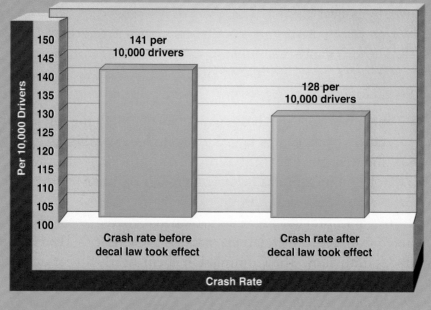

How Kyleigh's Law Affected Teen Crash Rates

Per 10,000 Drivers

141 per 10,000 drivers

128 per 10,000 drivers

Crash rate before decal law took effect

Crash rate after decal law took effect

Crash Rate

Taken from: Larry Higgs. "Study Finds Kyleigh's Law Has Reduced Teen Crashes." www.dailyrecord.com, October 23, 2012.

AAA [American Automobile Association] advocated for passage of the measure, believing that the new decals will be a great tool to keeping our roads and teens safer. The new decals, coupled with the new restrictions of the GDL, address the most dangerous driving habits of new drivers and the challenges to the enforcing [of] the provisions.

Preventing Profiling

Many of the objections over the decal program stem from concerns of profiling—it bears repeating that the law aims to prevent such action. Without the decals, law enforcement found it difficult to determine which drivers were subject to the restrictions of GDL. The decals serve as a tool for law enforcement to identify drivers who are in violation of the restrictions. The decals would only cause a driver to be pulled over if they do not obey the GDL restrictions; young drivers who follow the laws and drive safely have no need for concern.

It is clear that these new laws, like many changes before them, are fraught with opposition and concerns. With time and the proper education and enforcement these new restrictions will become a standard part of a teen's driving experience. AAA is committed to working with our partners to provide the necessary education to teens, their parents and law enforcement.

It is unfortunate that some have responded to the objections by offering a quick repeal of this important safety measure. AAA urges the Legislature to heed the months of hard, reasoned work done by

Jon Corzine, then New Jersey governor, speaks before signing the bill known as Kyleigh's Law in 2009, named in honor of sixteen-year-old Kyleigh D'Alessio, who was killed in a car accident when a teen was driving.

the study Commission. Give the law sufficient time to show its merits and improve safety. Let data and proven safety benefits guide the Legislature in its decision-making process.

EVALUATING THE AUTHOR'S ARGUMENTS:

Frederick L. Gruel contends that marking the license plates of drivers under age twenty-one with decals helps police to enforce laws and makes the roads safer for everyone. Are you persuaded by his argument? Why or why not?

Viewpoint

6

Cars Driven by Teens Should Not Be Marked with Decals

Alex Koroknay-Palicz

"There is zero justification for singling out new, young drivers [by using decals]."

Alex Koroknay-Palicz is the executive director of the National Youth Rights Association, an organization dedicated to defending the civil and human rights of young people in the United States. In the viewpoint that follows Koroknay-Palicz argues against a New Jersey law that requires decals to be displayed on cars driven by newly licensed youths. While the stickers are intended to help police enforce restricted-license laws, the author believes they make youths driving alone more vulnerable to sexual predators and other criminals. Other countries with similar laws require stickers for any newly licensed driver, not just those who are under twenty-one. Targeting youths in this way is unfair and unsafe, he maintains.

AS YOU READ, CONSIDER THE FOLLOWING QUESTIONS:
1. According to the author, what happened after a law was passed in Florida requiring rental cars to be marked with decals?
2. How many youths have joined the group NJ Teens Against 'Kyleigh's Law' Teen Driving Restrictions, according to Koroknay-Palicz?
3. Why does the author object to bans on teen drivers using cell phones?

A new law . . . in New Jersey . . . requires provisional drivers under 21 to put a red sticker on their license plate. The law, nicknamed Kyleigh's Law, after Kyleigh D'Alessio, who died in a car accident in 2006, is purported to make it easier for the police to enforce graduated driver's license provisions on new drivers. The law is designed to give the police probable cause to pull over vehicles displaying the red sticker. The law also includes changes to New Jersey's already fairly strict requirements for young people with provisional driver's licenses, stopping individuals under 21 from driving past 11 PM instead of midnight and stopping drivers from using all cell phones (whether hands free or not). This law also increases restrictions on the passengers a young driver can have in the car. This is the first state in the country to attempt to require new, young drivers to display a special tag or notice on their car identifying them as such.

This law raises a number of important questions, some of which are rather unsettling. First of all, why are only new drivers under 21 required to display this sticker? No evidence exists that shows new drivers over 21 are safer than other new drivers. If this law were about safety then surely all new drivers should have the same restrictions and have the same red sticker on the back of their car. Proponents of this law cite Canada, which has a similar identification for new drivers, but [its] law applies to all new drivers, not just new drivers under 21. The law is similar in Europe, where new drivers, of any age, have to display some special marking. There is zero justification for singling out new, young drivers. None.

An Unsettling Question

The plan was for the sticker to put a bullseye on the back of young people's cars, making them easier to pull over. The unsettling question we need to ask is, who else out there would like to easily identify young people driving alone? Our mind can conjure up many stalkers, criminals and sexual predators who could use this marking system to their advantage. Do we really want to put such a target on the cars of our youth?

New Jersey attorney, Gregg Trautmann, filed suit against the law hoping to stop it going into effect due to its safety concerns. His case lost the first round but he is working on an appeal.

Such concerns aren't unjustified fears. In the 90's a law in Florida requiring rental cars to display stickers identifying them as rentals

Studies have shown that a young person talking on a cell phone while driving is no more hazardous than a senior citizen driving and not talking on a cell phone.

led to the murders of nine people in the state. Criminals used those stickers to identify tourists who were often unsure of their surroundings and ran them off the road with the intent to rob them, or worse.

Because of concerns over the dangerous and discriminatory implications of this law, it . . . attracted a storm of criticism before it [had] even gone on the books. Nearly 30,000 have joined a group called "NJ Teens Against 'Kyleigh's Law' Teen Driving Restrictions" and over 9,000 members have joined a Facebook group named "Kyleigh's Law lets creepers know I'm young and alone." Thousands more have joined one of the other 14 Facebook pages created to oppose this law. The members of many threaten non-compliance with this law. The comment sections of news websites are overwhelmed with passionate comments of young people and parents upset over this law.

Lawmakers are starting to take notice. Assemblymen Robert Schroeder and Michael Patrick Carroll are already planning to introduce legislation to repeal the law. Carroll, who initially voted for the law, hadn't considered the law's negative implications for the safety of youth. He now is working to oppose it and has been impressed with the public outcry against it.

Opposition to the Scarlet Letter Sticker

My organization, the National Youth Rights Association, is calling upon all drivers over 21 in New Jersey to voluntarily put a red sticker on their license plate as a sign of solidarity with all the individuals under 21. Some have described our efforts as "sabotage" but we see it as showing support and solidarity with young people who have been singled out in such an egregious manner, letting them know they aren't alone and that people of all ages oppose this law. That's the point of it. If, however, it causes some sexual predator to think twice before following a car with a red sticker on it, then all the better.

This scarlet letter sticker is the most striking and unique part of this law, but there are questions about its other provisions as well. The

Opposition to Kyleigh's Law

Percent of nineteen–year–old college students who oppose Kyleigh's Law on the basis of increased sexual predation.

80%

Taken from: "Kyleigh's Law: Does It Protect or Further Endanger Teen Drivers?" *The Gleaner*, September 20, 2010.

law bans provisional license holders under 21 from using a cell phone entirely, no matter if they are talking, texting, or using a hands-free device. Obviously the last thing New Jersey wants a young girl to do after a creepy van spots the sticker and starts following her is to call for help.

Cell Phones

Talking on a cell phone while driving is certainly dangerous; it slows reaction times and distracts them from the road. But there is zero evidence that it is uniquely dangerous for young people. In fact studies show that a young person talking on a cellphone while driving is no different than a senior citizen not on a cell phone. Young people have naturally better reaction times and, no surprise, are far more accustomed to talking on the cell phone than grandpa. If there is anyone in this world who I'd want to drive and talk on a cell phone it is a teenager. Why then is New Jersey singling them out for this ban? Why also is Congress singling them out as well?

If this law was remotely based on science or on reality then all drivers, regardless of age, would not be allowed to drive while talking on a cell phone. Moreover, if we are so frightened by the reduced reaction times of teens on phones, then we should pass a law banning all people over 65 from driving period.

Of course as restrictions multiply ever faster on young drivers, our dangerous grandparents are left untouched. Despite reduced eye sight no law restricts the hours they can drive. Despite their problems with focus and attention, no law restricts how many passengers are in their car. Despite their problems with reflexes and reaction times, no law restricts whether they can use a cell phone. Why? Why does every feel-good, do-nothing law seeking to "keep us safe" only ever target young people? Because senior citizens vote.

While Kyleigh's Law is just one example of the recent trend of lumping 18–20-year-old adults in with teens, there is still one adult right they continue to enjoy—the right to vote. For all those out there opposed to this onerous new law, I encourage you to exercise this right and vote the bums out.

EVALUATING THE AUTHOR'S ARGUMENTS:

Alex Koroknay-Palicz is the executive director of the National Youth Rights Association. Describe how his credentials might inform his argument against the use of decals on cars driven by youths. Do you think that his credentials help make his argument convincing? Or do they make his argument seem biased? Explain.

Chapter 3

What Strategies Would Make Teen Driving Safer?

A teen gets a thumbs-up from her driving instructor. Advanced driving classes can make teen driving safer.

Viewpoint

1

Crash Rates May Be Higher for Teen Drivers Who Start School Earlier in the Morning

"Starting high school later in the morning may promote driver alertness by allowing teens to get more sleep at night."

E! Science News

Car accident rates are often higher for teen drivers who start school earlier in the morning, reports *E! Science News* in the following selection. According to a study published in the *Journal of Clinical Sleep Medicine*, researchers found a higher rate of crashes among teen drivers who started school at 7:20 in the morning in comparison to teens whose classes started at least an hour later. Another study found that teens who received an extra hour of sleep each night due to delayed school start times performed better on tests requiring attention. This data suggests that delaying the time that classes start could make driving safer for teens. *E! Science News* is a Web magazine that provides access to the latest breakthroughs in popular science.

AS YOU READ, CONSIDER THE FOLLOWING QUESTIONS:

1. According to a study published in the *Journal of Clinical Sleep Medicine* cited by *E! Science News*, how do the weekday car crash rates for teens in Virginia Beach, Virginia, compare with the car crash rates in Chesapeake, Virginia?
2. How much sleep does the average teen need each night, according to the American Academy of Sleep Medicine, as cited by the author?
3. According to the author, what changes in their biology make it difficult for teens to get enough sleep on school nights?

A study in the April 15 issue of the *Journal of Clinical Sleep Medicine* shows increased automobile crash rates among teen drivers who start school earlier in the morning. Results indicate that in 2008 the weekday crash rate for 16- to 18-year-olds was about 41 percent higher in Virginia Beach, Va., where high school classes began at 7:20–7:25 AM, than in adjacent Chesapeake, Va., where classes started at 8:40–8:45 AM. There were 65.8 automobile crashes for every 1,000 teen drivers in Virginia Beach, and 46.6 crashes for every 1,000 teen drivers in Chesapeake. Similar results were found for 2007, when the weekday crash rate for Virginia Beach teens (71.2) was 28 percent higher than for Chesapeake teens (55.6). In a secondary analysis that evaluated only the traditional school months of September 2007 through June 2008, the weekday crash rate for teen drivers was 25 percent higher in Virginia Beach (80.0) than in Chesapeake (64.0). An investigation of traffic congestion in the neighboring cities did not reveal differences that might account for the teen crash findings.

> **FAST FACT**
>
> The circadian rhythm is a kind of internal clock that regulates cycles of sleeping and waking in humans and animals.

"We were concerned that Virginia Beach teens might be sleep restricted due to their early rise times and that this could eventuate in an increased crash rate," said lead author Robert Vorona, MD,

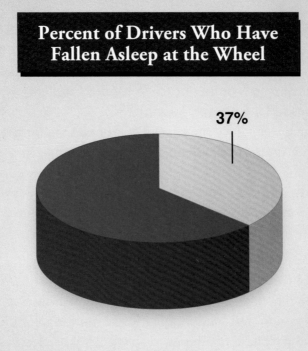

Percent of Drivers Who Have Fallen Asleep at the Wheel

37%

Taken from: *Sleep in America*. National Sleep Foundation, 2005.

associate professor of internal medicine at Eastern Virginia Medical School in Norfolk, Va. "The study supported our hypothesis, but it is important to note that this study does not prove cause and effect. We are planning to perform subsequent studies to follow up on these results and to investigate other potential ramifications of early high school start times."

According to the American Academy of Sleep Medicine, the average teen needs a little more than nine hours of sleep each night. However, chronic sleep restriction is a common problem among teens. During adolescence, a biological change shifts the typical onset of sleepiness later at night. This delay can make it a challenge for teens to get enough sleep when they have to wake up early for school.

Vorona says that starting high school later in the morning may promote driver alertness by allowing teens to get more sleep at night.

"We believe that high schools should take a close look at having later start times to align with circadian rhythms in teens and to allow for longer sleep times," he said. "Too many teens in this country obtain insufficient sleep. Increasingly, the literature suggests that this may lead to problematic consequences including mood disorders, academic difficulties and behavioral issues."

Another study in the April issue of the *Journal of Clinical Sleep Medicine* suggests that delaying school start times by one hour could enhance students' cognitive performance by improving their attention level and increasing their rate of performance, as well as reducing their mistakes and impulsivity. The Israeli study of 14-year-old eighth-grade students found that the teens slept about 55 minutes longer each night and performed better on tests that require attention when their school start time was delayed by one hour.

Vorona's study involved data provided by the Virginia Department of Motor Vehicles. In Virginia Beach, there were 12,916 registered drivers between 16 and 18 years of age in 2008, and these teen drivers were involved in 850 crashes. In Chesapeake there were 8,459 teen drivers and 394 automobile accidents. The researchers report that the two adjoining cities have similar demographics, including racial composition and per-capita income.

A 2011 study showed that teen drivers who start school later in the morning have fewer auto accidents and do better in school because they get more sleep.

Further analysis by time of day found that, in the morning, the teen crash rates peaked when students would be commuting to school, from 7 AM to 7:59 AM for Virginia Beach and 8 AM to 8:59 AM for Chesapeake. Teen crash rates were highest in the afternoon hours, from 2 PM to 6 PM in Virginia Beach, where schools dismissed at about 2 PM, and from 4 PM to 7 PM in Chesapeake, where schools dismissed between 3 PM and 3:45 PM.

EVALUATING THE AUTHOR'S ARGUMENTS:

Robert Vorona, the lead author of the study that found that car crash rates may be higher for teen drivers who start school earlier in the morning, cautions that this study does not prove cause and effect. Thus, he wants to perform further follow-up research. Do you agree that further studies are needed? Why or why not? Could there be other factors affecting crash rates for teen drivers who receive less sleep? Explain.

Car Key Jams Teen Drivers' Cell Phone and Texting

"Zhou and Curry... came up with the idea of blocking cell phone usage via a vehicle ignition key."

Newswise

The following selection explores a technological solution to the problem of distracted driving for teens: an ignition key that prevents texting or talking on a cell phone while the car is running. Developed by engineer Xuesong Zhou and physician Wally Curry, the key has a wireless connection to the driver's cell phone. Starting the car's engine requires the driver to release a switch on the key, placing it in a mode that blocks nonemergency use of the cell phone. Newswise is an online newswire service.

AS YOU READ, CONSIDER THE FOLLOWING QUESTIONS:
1. According to Xuesong Zhou, as cited in the viewpoint, what percentage of teen drivers are talking or texting on cell phones at any given time?
2. What is the difference between the teen and adult versions of the Key2SafeDriving system, according to Newswise?
3. What incident, according to the author, inspired Wally Curry to create a system that would prevent the use of cell phones while driving?

Uuniversity of Utah researchers have developed an automobile ignition key that prevents teenagers from talking on cell phones or sending text messages while driving.

The university has obtained provisional patents and licensed the invention "Key2SafeDriving" to a private company that hopes to see it on the market within six months [by mid-2009] at a cost of less than $50 per key plus a yet-undetermined monthly service fee.

"The key to safe driving is to avoid distraction," says Xuesong Zhou, an assistant professor of civil and environmental engineering who co-invented the system with Wally Curry, a University of Utah graduate now practicing medicine in Hays, Kan. "We want to provide a simple, cost-effective solution to improve driving safety."

Zhou notes that "at any given time, about 6 percent of travelers on the road are talking on a cell phone while driving. Also at any given time, 10 percent of teenagers who are driving are talking or texting." Studies have shown drivers using cell phones are about four times more likely to get in a crash than other drivers.

"As a parent, you want to improve driving safety for your teenagers," he says. "You also want to reduce your insurance costs for your teen drivers. Using our system you can prove that teen drivers are not talking while driving, which can significantly reduce the risk of getting into a car accident."

If things go as planned, the Key2SafeDriving system won't be sold directly to consumers by a manufacturer, but instead the technology may be licensed to cell phone service providers to include in their service plans, says Ronn Hartman, managing partner of Accendo LC.

The Kaysville, Utah, company provides early-stage business consulting and "seed funding." It has licensed the Key2SafeDriving technology from the University of Utah and is working to manufacture and commercialize it.

Hartman envisions gaining automobile and insurance industry backing so that Key2SafeDriving data on cell phone use (or non-use) while driving can be compiled into a "safety score" and sent monthly to insurance companies, which then would provide discounts to motorists with good scores. The score also could include data recorded via Global Positioning System (GPS) satellites on the driver's speeding, rapid braking or running of lights, which are calculated by comparing the driver's position with a database of maps, speed limits, stop lights and so on.

How Key2SafeDriving Works

The system includes a device that encloses a car key, one for each teen driver or family member. The device connects wirelessly with each key user's cell phone via either Bluetooth or RFID (radio-frequency identification) technologies.

FAST FACT

Fatal car crashes account for at least 30 percent of teen deaths in the United States, according to federal statistics.

To turn on the engine, the driver must either slide the key out or push a button to release it. Then the device sends a signal to the driver's cell phone, placing it in "driving mode" and displaying a "stop" sign on the phone's display screen.

While in driving mode, teen drivers cannot use their cell phones to talk or send text messages, except for calling 911 or other numbers pre-approved by the parents—most likely the parents' own cell numbers.

Incoming calls and texts are automatically answered with a message saying, "I am driving now. I will call you later when I arrive at the destination safely."

When the engine is turned off, the driver slides the key back into the device, which sends a "car stopped" signal to the cell phone, returning it to normal communication mode.

University of Utah researchers developed an automobile ignition key (called the Key2SafeDriving system) that disables a cell phone while the car's engine is running, thus preventing teens (and others) from using their cell phones while driving.

The device can't be "tricked" by turning the phone off and on again because the phone will receive the "driving mode" signal whenever the car key is extended.

Adult drivers cannot text or use a handheld cell phone, but the Key2SafeDriving system does allow them to talk using a hands-free cell phone " even though studies by University of Utah psychologists indicate hands-free phones are just as distracting as handheld phones.

Curry agrees that driving while talking on any cell phone "is not safe," but he says the inventors have to face the practical issue of whether adults would buy a product to completely block their cell phone use while driving.

Limiting some cell calls by adults "is a step in the right direction," he says.

Zhou says the goal for adults is to improve safety by encouraging them to reduce the time they spend talking while driving. The encouragement could come in the form of insurance discounts by insurers, who would receive monthly scores from Key2SafeDriving showing how well an adult driver avoided talking while driving.

An Invention Is Born

The new invention began with Curry, a Salt Lake City native who graduated from the University of Utah with an accounting degree and premedical training in 1993. He returned from the Medical College of Wisconsin for his surgical residency in urology at University Hospital during 1998–2003. He now is a urologist in Hays, Kan.

His concern with driving-while-talking began because, as a doctor, "the hospital is calling me all the time on my cell phone when I'm driving."

One day while driving home, he saw a teenage girl texting while driving, making him worry about his 12- and 14-year-old daughters, who are approaching driving age.

"I thought, this is crazy, there has got to be something to stop this, because not only is she putting people at risk, but so was I," Curry says. "It struck me pretty hard that something should be done."

Curry's initial idea was a GPS system to detect a moving cell phone and disable it when it moved at driving speeds. Meanwhile, someone else developed a similar system based on the same idea. But it cannot distinguish if the cell phone user is driving a car or is a passenger in a moving car, bus or train" a problem overcome by Key2SafeDriving.

In early 2008, Curry called Larry Reaveley, a civil engineering professor at the University of Utah, who suggested Curry contact Zhou, a specialist in "intelligent" transportation systems. Zhou and Curry then came up with the idea of blocking cell phone usage via a vehicle ignition key.

Zhou, a native of Liuzhou, China, joined the University of Utah faculty in early 2007. He received his Ph.D. degree from the University of Maryland in 2004. He has worked for a California company that sold a product that provides traffic information to motorists using GPS satellites.

EVALUATING THE AUTHOR'S ARGUMENTS:

The inventors profiled in this viewpoint maintain that a car key that prevents cell phone use while driving will significantly cut down on accidents involving teen drivers. Do you agree? Or do you think that there are better ways to reduce the risks for young drivers? Use evidence from the viewpoints in this volume in defending your answer.

Teen Activism Makes Teen Driving Safer

Liza Barth

"Messages about smart driving mean a lot more when we hear them from other teens."

Teen activism can encourage teenagers to be more responsible while they are driving, according the author Liza Barth in the following viewpoint. The author describes the work of teen activist Laura Saldivar, a sixteen-year-old student who works with many organizations to spread awareness on the issue of safe driving. Barth writes for Consumer Reports News.

AS YOU READ, CONSIDER THE FOLLOWING QUESTIONS:
1. What tragedy in Laura Saldivar's life occurred that inspired her to form a safe-driving group, according to Barth?
2. What are some of the safe-driving programs Saldivar has participated in, according to the author?
3. What was the Allstate pledge trying to prevent teens from doing while driving, according to the author?

Laura Saldivar is a typical 16-year-old student, but her initiative and actions to help spread awareness on the issue of safe driving are anything but typical. The teen from Algonquin, Illinois, started getting involved six years ago at the ripe age of 10. She knows a bit about driver safety from her dad, since he is a driver education teacher, but the death of a cousin from distracted driving served as an inspiration to form a safe driving group at the local high school, long before she was a student there. The Jacobs Safety Initiative (named after her high school) began in 2006 and Saldivar hasn't stopped working for the cause since.

> ## FAST FACT
>
> According to *Scholastic Choices*, speeding causes nearly 40 percent of fatal crashes involving teens, and 87 percent of teens admit to speeding.

Her resume of initiatives is long and impressive—she currently serves on the Teen Distracted Driving Prevention Leadership Team for the National Organization for Youth Safety (NOYS), Students

Teens raise awareness of the high rate of deaths in auto accidents in a rally supporting the Keep the Drive movement.

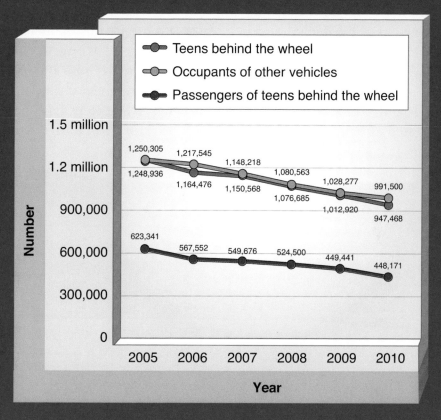

People Involved in Police–Reported Crashes with Teens Behind the Wheel (2005–2010)

Total number of people involved in 2010: 2,387,139
Total number of police-reported crashes in 2010: 887,233

Legend:
- Teens behind the wheel
- Occupants of other vehicles
- Passengers of teens behind the wheel

Teens behind the wheel: 1,250,305 (2005); 1,217,545 (2006); 1,148,218 (2007); 1,080,563 (2008); 1,028,277 (2009); 991,500 (2010)

Occupants of other vehicles: 1,248,936 (2005); 1,164,476 (2006); 1,150,568 (2007); 1,076,685 (2008); 1,012,920 (2009); 947,468 (2010)

Passengers of teens behind the wheel: 623,341 (2005); 567,552 (2006); 549,676 (2007); 524,500 (2008); 449,441 (2009); 448,171 (2010)

Number (Y-axis): 0; 300,000; 600,000; 900,000; 1.2 million; 1.5 million

Year (X-axis): 2005, 2006, 2007, 2008, 2009, 2010

Taken from: National Automotive Sampling System, General Estimates System (NASS-GES). National Highway Traffic Safety Administration. NASS-GES includes a representative sample of police-reported crashes on a traffic way causing property damage, injury, or death. The NASS-GES was designed to provide national estimates of crash trends.

Against Destructive Decisions (SADD) Illinois State Board, and Teen Safe Driving Coalition, among others. She has hosted leadership summits to help mobilize youth, worked with Allstate to get teens to thumbprint and pledge not to text and drive and implemented over fifty different projects and she isn't stopping there. In March [2011], her team will host a teen safety driving conference with 400 youths as well as state police, U.S representatives, the Illinois Secretary of State and victims in attendance. She is also racking up frequent flier miles traveling around the country to speak at a variety of conferences.

She believes in the peer-to-peer model of awareness, because teens listen to their peers. She says they don't think it will happen to them, but it took losing people for them to understand.

She received her driver's license last April and always drives with her phone off and out of sight and doesn't believe in the new phenomenon of having a designated texter and her friends know never to text and drive with her in the car.

Laura is just one of a many teens around the country who are working in their communities and schools to bring awareness, change, and leadership to the issue of distracted driving. While teens have been targeted as being part of the problem, they can also be part of the solution and help saves lives.

EVALUATING THE AUTHOR'S ARGUMENTS:

Do you agree with author Liza Barth that teen activists can persuade youths to be more responsible as drivers? Why or why not?

Viewpoint

4

Should We Increase Requirements for Teenage Drivers?

John O'Neil

"Parental involvement is crucial to making graduated licensing systems work."

Parents should be required to attend a driving safety class before their child receives a driver's license, argues John O'Neil in the following viewpoint. When states adopt this simple requirement, teen driver crash rates fall, he contends. Although some parents complain about having to take a class, the data proves that parental involvement with their children's driving instruction reduces the number of accidents that cause injury or death. O'Neil is a writer and editor for the *New York Times*.

AS YOU READ, CONSIDER THE FOLLOWING QUESTIONS:

1. By what percent does just one passenger raise the risk of an accident for a teen driver, according to O'Neil?
2. According to the author, how likely are teen drivers to use seatbelts if their parents monitor their driving?
3. What did Connecticut police notice after their state began requiring a safety class for the parents of teen drivers, according to O'Neil?

P arents, is your work as an unpaid driving instructor done when your teenager gets a license? If you think so, here are some statistics that Pam Fischer, who oversees the New Jersey Teen Safe Driving Coalition, says you should know:

- For teenage drivers, a single passenger raises the risk of a crash by 50 percent and doubles the risk of the driver dying in a crash; three passengers increase the risk of a crash by 200 percent.
- Teenagers whose parents set rules and monitor their independent driving are half as likely to get into a crash as teenagers with no parental supervision; and they're 71 percent less likely to drive while intoxicated and 50 percent more likely to use their seat belts.

Ms. Fischer's safe driving coalition lobbied for a bill that was passed by the New Jersey Legislature in late December 2011 that would have required parents to attend a driving safety class before their child could be eligible for a license. (The bill was vetoed by Gov. Chris Christie, along with almost 50 other bills in what amounted to a collective rebuke of legislators for procrastinating, but its sponsors plan to reintroduce it this year.)

FAST FACT

More than three hundred thousand teens are injured in car crashes each year in the United States.

The bill, which also lengthened the permit period and increased the required hours of practice, was an attempt to have the law catch up with the reality that driver's education depends on parents more than ever, but without any mechanism for getting them engaged, Ms. Fischer said. The proposed change comes in the form of graduated drivers licensing, or G.D.L., under which new drivers face periods with curfews, passenger limits or other restrictions. States that have adopted these requirements have seen their crash rates for teenagers drop by 10 to 30 percent, according to Russ Rader of the Insurance Institute for Highway Safety.

But while G.D.L. laws carry penalties for violating the restrictions, their effectiveness does not come primarily from the threat of arrest, Mr.

Many contend that parental involvement in their children's driver education—even at a minimal level—reduces crash rates for teen drivers.

Rader said. "Parental involvement is crucial to making graduated licensing systems work," he said, "because parents are the first line enforcers of the law."

To Ms. Fischer, what the graduated licensing does is "establish some minimum standards to help you really help your teens" as they transition from supervised to independent driving. "It gives parents the hammer," she said, "because when a teen challenges a restriction, parents can say they have that law backing them up."

But parents can't use that hammer if they don't understand it. Connecticut adopted a parent safety class requirement in 2008. The law is still producing some grousing from "parents who see it as one more hoop to jump through," said Bill Seymour, the director of communications for the state's Department of Motor Vehicles. But, he said, "the numbers are clear—deaths are dramatically down, accidents with injuries are dramatically down."

State figures show that crashes in Connecticut in which 16- or 17-year-old drivers were considered a contributing factor fell by 28 percent in the two years after the rules went into effect.

A Department of Motor Vehicles report in 2011 showed that the police have become more aggressive about making arrests for violations of curfew or passenger limit laws, with convictions of teenagers rising for those offenses—but falling sharply for speeding, not using seat belts, distracted driving and driving under the influence. And the percentage of 16- and 17-year-olds with licenses has fallen, although Mr. Seymour said that the economy has likely played a role, as well as the new laws.

Ms. Fischer has another response to parents who are reluctant to part with yet another 90 minutes of their time. "My son plays hockey," she said. "There's a mandatory parent meeting before the start of the season, and he can't play if I don't go."

"What's a higher priority?" she asked. "He can get hurt playing hockey, but has a far higher risk of dying in a car crash."

EVALUATING THE AUTHOR'S ARGUMENTS:

In the previous viewpoint, Liza Barth argues that youths can be motivated by their peers to become better drivers. In this viewpoint, however, John O'Neil contends that parental involvement in their children's driver education—even at a minimal level—reduces crash rates for teen drivers. In your opinion, which tactic is more effective: peer influence or parental involvement? Explain.

Facts About Teen Driving

Editor's note: These facts can be used in reports to add credibility when making important points or claims.

The US Department of Transportation reports that more than three thousand American teens die each year in car accidents, accounting for nearly half of all teen deaths in the United States.

Motor vehicle crashes kill nearly five times as many teens as cancer or poisoning, reports teendriversource.org.

For each teen killed in a car crash, about a hundred more are injured, according to the Department of Transportation.

Seventy percent of young drivers who drink and then die in a car crash were not wearing seatbelts.

According to Students Against Destructive Decisions (SADD), 20 percent of teens say that their parents have never spoken to them about driving safety.

According to the AAA Foundation for Traffic Safety:
- crash rates per mile driven for teens are four times higher than for adults;
- teens are 50 percent more likely to crash in the first month of driving than after a year;
- a survey of a thousand teens found that 46 percent texted while driving, and 51 percent talked on the phone while driving.

Carnegie Mellon University reports that driving while using a cell phone reduces the amount of brain activity associated with driving by 37 percent.

Forty percent of US teens say that they have been in a car when the driver used a cell phone in a way that put people in danger, according to a Pew Research Center survey.

Distracted drivers are four times more likely to have an accident, asserts Try Safety First.

According to the National Highway Traffic Safety Administration:

- Sixteen percent of all distracted-driving crashes involve youths under twenty;
- people who text while driving are twenty-three times more likely to crash;
- sending or reading a text takes a driver's eyes off the road for 4.6 seconds. At fifty-five miles per hour, that is the equivalent of driving the length of a football field blind.
- teenage drivers and passengers are among the least likely to wear seatbelts.

According to the University of Michigan and the US Department of Transportation:

- In 2010, 28 percent of all sixteen-year-olds had driver's licenses, compared with 44 percent in 1980;
- in 2010, 45 percent of all seventeen-year-olds had driver's licenses, compared with 66 percent in 1980.
- in 2010, 61 percent of all eighteen-year-olds had driver's licenses, compared with 75 percent in 1980.

Allstate Insurance reports that 74 percent of US teens support comprehensive graduated driver's licensing laws.

Organizations to Contact

The editors have compiled the following list of organizations concerned with the issues debated in this book. The descriptions are derived from materials provided by the organizations. All have publications or information available for interested readers. The list was compiled on the date of publication of the present volume; the information provided here may change. Be aware that many organizations take several weeks or longer to respond to inquiries, so allow as much time as possible for the receipt of requested materials.

AAA Foundation for Traffic Safety
607 Fourteenth St. NW, Ste. 201
Washington, DC 20005
(202) 638-5944
fax: (202) 638-5943
e-mail: info@aaafoundation.org
website: www.aaafoundation.org

The AAA Foundation for Traffic Safety is a nonprofit educational and research organization dedicated to saving lives and reducing injuries on the roads. Since 1947 the foundation has funded hundreds of projects designed to discover the causes of traffic accidents, prevent them, and minimize injuries when they do occur. Its major research areas include: teen driver safety, road safety, and safety culture. The home page includes a link to "Keys2Drive: The AAA Guide to Teen Driver Safety," featuring information on the driver's licensing process and pointers on becoming a safer, more skilled driver.

National Highway Traffic Safety Administration (NHTSA)
1200 New Jersey Ave. SE, West Bldg.
Washington, DC 20590
(202) 266-4000; toll-free: (888) 327-4236
website: www.nhtsa.gov

Part of the US Department of Transportation, the NHTSA was established in 1970 as the successor to the National Highway Safety Bureau. Its goal is to reduce deaths, injuries, and economic losses resulting from vehicular crashes by setting and enforcing safety standards for motor vehicles and by assisting states to conduct effective highway safety programs. The NHTSA also conducts research on driver behavior and offers consumers information on motor vehicle safety. Its website includes links to articles, reports, and studies on driver education, distracted driving, impaired driving, and related topics.

National Organizations for Youth Safety (NOYS)
7371 Atlas Walk Way, #109
Gainesville, VA 20155
(828) 367-6697
website: www.noys.org

NOYS is an alliance of over sixty youth-serving organizations—including nonprofit groups, businesses, and government agencies—with the aim of promoting safe and healthy behaviors among American youth. The coalition focuses on issues such as teen drug abuse, teen obesity, school bullying, and teen driver distractions. The NOYS home page provides links to multimedia traffic safety resources, including a texting-while-driving simulator video, as well as links to reports and articles such as "Teen Driver Deaths Increase, Study Says," and *Distracted Driving: What Research Shows and What States Can Do.*

National Youth Rights Association (NYRA)
1101 Fifteenth St. NW, Ste. 200
Washington, DC 20005
(202) 835-1719
website: www.youthrights.org

The NYRA is a national nonprofit youth-led organization dedicated to fighting for the civil rights and liberties of young people. Its mission centers on challenging age discrimination against young people, both in law and in attitudes, and it seeks to create a world where people are judged by talent, intelligence, and integrity rather than birth date. Lowering the drinking age and repealing curfew laws are two specific areas of advocacy. The NYRA website includes an online library, a state-by-state guide on driving age, and a database with links to news articles such as "Research Shows That Teens in No Hurry to Be Behind Wheel," and "Graduated Driver's Licenses: Opinions, Policies Vary."

Partners for Safe Teen Driving
Prince William County Public Schools
PO Box 389, Manassas, VA 20108
(800) 609-2680
fax: (703) 791-7378
e-mail: info@pwnet.org
website: www.safeteendriving.org

An arm of the Virginia Association of Driver Education and Traffic Safety, Partners for Safe Teen Driving is a community health initiative aimed at reducing the number of injuries and fatalities due to teen car accidents. With multimedia awareness campaigns and instructional materials, this initiative teaches parents and teens about risky behaviors, new driving techniques, licensing laws, and safe driving practices. Materials featured at the website include the articles "Safe Driving Basics" and "Distracted, Drunk, and Drugged Driving," as well as the video "It Can Wait" and links to public service announcements on safe driving.

Students Against Destructive Decisions (SADD)
255 Main St., Marlborough, MA 01752
(877) 723-3562
fax: (508) 481-5759
e-mail: info@sadd.org
website: www.sadd.org

Originally known as Students Against Drunk Driving, SADD expanded its mission in 1997 and changed its name to Students Against Destructive Decisions. Today SADD is a peer-led education, prevention, and activism organization dedicated to preventing teens from making harmful choices, particularly drinking, drug abuse, risky and impaired driving, teen violence, and teen suicide. Its website includes links to research on teen driving, articles, and editorials, including "The Gift of a Lifetime—Friends Don't Let Friends Drive Dangerously."

Try Safety First, Inc.
1948 Miniball Ridge
Marietta, GA 30064
(770) 652-4517
e-mail: admin@trysafetyfirst.com
website: www.trysafetyfirst.com

Try Safety First is a company that develops wireless communication safety systems. Its signature product is the OCK, created for the purpose of providing a solution to the cell phone/distracted driving epidemic. The company maintains that laws against cell phone use while driving are ineffective and believes that embedding distraction prevention and safety protocols into cell phones is a better way to prevent cell phone–related traffic accidents. The "Try Safety First White Paper" is available as a free download at its website.

**University of North Carolina Highway
Safety Research Center (HSRC)**
730 Martin Luther King Jr. Blvd., CB# 3430
Chapel Hill, NC 27599-3430
(919) 962-2203
fax: (919) 962-8710
e-mail: info@hsrc.unc.edu
website: www.hsrc.unc.edu

Established in 1965, the HSRC is a research institute that has helped to shape the field of transportation safety. The center's goal is to improve the safety, security, and efficiency of roads and highways through research, evaluation, and education. Its website provides a variety of resources to the public, including an online research library, highway safety data and tools, a list of national-level information clearinghouses, as well as links to articles and editorials on teen driving.

US Department of Transportation
1200 New Jersey Ave. SE
Washington, DC 20590
(855) 368-4200
website: www.dot.gov

Established in 1967, this cabinet department serves the United States with its efforts of ensuring a fast, safe, efficient, accessible, and convenient transportation system that enhances the quality of life for the American people. Available through a link at its website is the National Transportation Library, which provides access to various articles, reports, and studies, including "Teen Driver Cell Phone Blocker" and "Activating Teens to Prevent Traffic Crashes."

US National Library of Medicine (NLM)
8600 Rockville Pike
Bethesda, MD 20894
(888) 346-3656
fax: (301) 402-1384
website: www.nlm.nih.gov

Stationed on the campus of the National Institutes of Health in Maryland, the NLM is the world's largest biomedical library. It houses a vast print collection and produces electronic information resources on a wide variety of topics, all made available to people around the globe. The NLM also supports and conducts research, development, and training in biomedicine and health information technology. PubMed and MedicinePlus are two of the NLM's online databases. Articles available through these databases include "Safe Driving for Teens," and "Do Video Games Promote Reckless Driving in Certain Teens?"

For Further Reading

Books

Beradelli, Phil. *Safe Young Drivers: A Guide for Parents and Teens*. 4th ed. Vienna, VA: Mountain Lake, 2008. This book offers step-by-step guidance for both parents and teens on responsible driving. It includes structured lessons and allows new drivers to experience potential dangers in a controlled environment so they can practice needed skills.

Hayes, Anne Marie. *Three Keys to Keeping Your Teen Alive: Lessons for Surviving the First Year of Driving*. New York: Morgan James, 2011. This book, written for both teens and parents, includes twenty-five structured driving lessons; discussions on distracted, drowsy, and impaired driving; car maintenance and repair tips; and compelling stories about real teen drivers.

Jackson, Trish. *Don't Text and Drive: 22 Safe Driving Tips for Teenage Drivers*. Seattle: CreateSpace, 2011. A writer who grew up on a farm in Zimbabwe, Africa, combines humor, illustrations, and facts in this guidebook that aims to keep teenage drivers safe on the roads.

Mullarky, D.K. *Get on the Bus! Because You Can't Drive*. 2nd ed. Bloomington, IN: iUniverse, 2012. The author—both a driver and a car-accident survivor—combines humor and practical advice in this book that encourages drivers to revisit their own driving habits.

Roy-Bornstein, Carolyn. *Crash: A Mother, a Son, and the Journey from Grief to Gratitude*. Guilford, CT: Globe Pequot, 2012. The author, a pediatrician, tells the story of what happened after her teenage son and his girlfriend were hit by a teen drunk driver. Although her son survived the accident, bleeding in his brain caused memory loss and personality changes.

Stalder, Erika. *In the Driver's Seat: A Girl's Guide to Her First Car*. San Francisco: Zest, 2009. Written for the novice young woman driver, this is a guide to buying, understanding, and maintaining a first car. It includes tips on fixing minor problems, choosing a mechanic, and surviving emergency situations.

Periodicals and Internet Sources

Alcindor, Yamiche. "Research Shows That Teens in No Hurry to Be Behind Wheel," *USA Today*, March 15, 2012.

Austin, Michael. "Texting While Driving: How Dangerous Is It?," *Car and Driver Magazine*, June 2009.

Beattie, Ann. "Joyride, with Bullhorn," *New York*, June 27, 2011.

Boyerand, Barbara, and Angelo Fichera. "N.J. High Court Upholds License-Plate Decals for Young Drivers," *Philadelphia Inquirer*, August 6, 2012.

Copeland, Larry. "Technology Tackles Teen Drivers' Phone Distractions," *USA Today*, January 12, 2012.

DiConsiglio, John. "He Drove Drunk—and Someone Died," *Scholastic Choices*, September 2011.

Elejalde-Ruiz, Alexia. "Can Teens Prevent Friends from Texting and Driving?," *Chicago Tribune*, May 30, 2012.

Esposito, Stefano. "Fewer Teens Desperate to Drive—Is the Internet the Reason?," *Chicago Sun-Times*, January 12, 2012.

Gorzelany, Jim. " Social Media Trumps Driving Among Today's Teens," *Forbes*, January 23, 2012.

Halsey, Ashley, III. "Laws Are Not Dissuading Drivers from Texting, Report Finds," *Washington Post*, September 29, 2010.

Hirsch, Jerry. "Teen Drivers Dangerously Divide Their Attention," *Los Angeles Times*, August 3, 2012.

Jackson, Nancy Mann. "Dn't txt n drv: Why You Should Disconnect While Driving," *Current Health Teens*, March 2011.

Kent, Debra. "Crash-Proof Your Teen: There's a New Way to Prep Your Child to Get Behind the Wheel. Here, the Info Every Parent Needs," *Good Housekeeping*, May 2010.

Laliberte, Richard. "Driven to Distraction: Teens Behind the Wheel," *Family Circle*, November 1, 2010.

Mays, Kelsey. "Teen Safe Driving 101: Understanding Common Mistakes Young Drivers Make Can Help Them Avoid Accidents," *Chicago Tribune*, December 4, 2011.

McCluggage, Denise. "They're Show-Offs, Not Thrill Seekers," *Auto Week*, March 5, 2012.

Mohn, Tanya. "The Mixed Bag of Driver Education," *New York Times*, June 22, 2012.

National Sleep Foundation. "Young People More Likely to Drive Drowsy," Drowsydriving.org, November 9, 2012. http://drowsy-driving.org/2012/11/young-people-more-likely-to-drive-drowsy/.

Provano, Joel. "Risky Business: Teens Driving with Other Teens," *Atlanta Journal-Constitution*, January 24, 2012.

Risch, Dan. "Building Better Drivers," *Odyssey*, September 2009.

Roy, Rex. "Teaching Teen Drivers," *Popular Mechanics*, June 2011.

Swartsell, Nick. "Cities Disagree on Texting-Driving Ban," *New York Times*, October 28, 2012.

Tampa Bay (FL) Times. "NOW READ THIS. IT CAN REALLY WAIT," October 8, 2012.

Tracey, Michael. "Dead Kids Make Bad Laws," *Reason*, June 1, 2011.

Wallace, Stephen. "Reindeer Games: Holiday Hooliganism Determines Danger," Students Against Destructive Decisions, November 28, 2011. http://sadd.org/oped/reindeer_games.htm.

Websites

Keep the Drive (www.keepthedrive.com). Keep the Drive is a teen-led movement that educates youth about safe and smart driving. The movement's home page features several research reports on teen driving, information about graduated driver's licenses, and links to detailed information about teen driving laws for each state in the United States.

TeenDriverSource (www.teendriversource.org). This website is provided by a team of researchers and educators from the Center for Injury Research and Prevention at the Children's Hospital of Philadelphia Research Institute. It includes links to news articles, downloadable fact sheets, and research reports such as "Driving: Through the Eyes of Teens."

Tire Rack Street Survival (www.streetsurvival.org). With the help of corporate sponsors BMW of North America and the Tire Rack, Tire Rack Street Survival is a safe-teen-driving education program offered at dozens of high schools throughout the United States. The "Latest News" tab gives readers online access to articles on teen driving from various newspapers and magazines.

Index

Picture Credits

© AP Images, 53

© AP Images/Press of Atlantic City, Danny Drake, 18

© AP Photo/Bob Child, 40

© AP Photo/Mel Evans, 63

© AP Photo/Press-Register, Michelle Rolls, 75

© Art Directors & TRIP/Alamy, 49

© Clark Brennan/Alamy, 12

© Cusp/SuperStock, 38

© Drive Images/Alamy, 31

© Gale, Cengage Learning, 13, 17, 26, 33, 37, 43, 47, 57, 62, 69, 74, 85

© David McNew/Getty Images, 44

© PRNewsFoto/The Allstate Foundation, Elizabeth Flores, 84

© Purcell Pictures, Inc./Alamy, 67

© Tetra Images/Alamy, 10, 22, 89

© Tom Williams/Roll Call/Getty Images, 25

© Visions of America, LLC/Alamy, 58

© Lisa F. Young/Alamy, 71

© ZUMA Press, Inc./Alamy, 80